# RECOVERY FROM
## BLOW

# RECOVERY FROM BLOW

## Behind the Scenes of the Movie, Blow

KRISTINA SUNSHINE JUNG

RECOVERY FROM BLOW
BEHIND THE SCENES OF THE MOVIE, BLOW

iUniverse books may be ordered through booksellers or by contacting:

iUniverse
1663 Liberty Drive
Bloomington, IN 47403
www.iuniverse.com
1-800-Authors (1-800-288-4677)

Because of the dynamic nature of the Internet, any web addresses or
links contained in this book may have changed since publication and
may no longer be valid. The views expressed in this work are solely those
of the author and do not necessarily reflect the views of the publisher,
and the publisher hereby disclaims any responsibility for them.

Any people depicted in stock imagery provided by Getty Images are
models, and such images are being used for illustrative purposes only.
Certain stock imagery © Getty Images.

ISBN: 978-1-5320-6247-6 (sc)
ISBN: 978-1-5320-6245-2 (hc)
ISBN: 978-1-5320-6246-9 (e)

Library of Congress Control Number: 2018913686

Print information available on the last page.

iUniverse rev. date: 11/15/2018

# CONTENTS

# PREFACE

# THE REAL STORY
# BEHIND BLOW

B ehind the scenes, the real players, the inside story of the power of the game. How it all rose to prominence and crumbled behind wars, cocaine, money, jealousy, envy, and greed; far beyond your imagination.

As a dream with nightmares...

Awakening to reality no longer questioning the should of, could of, would of. Only a feeling of peace. No longer feeling the desperation or urge for the drug nor the life style.

As you follow the pages throughout this book, think of it as a path, a path with twists, turns, and crossroads. When making decisions at a crossroad, you must choose to take the path to the light or the path to darkness. While on this journey you may see yourself within the pages of this book, or perhaps someone you may know.

It has taken years of strength to relive the past in the writing of this story after the movie Blow, or after blow, whatever it may be. Staying on the road to recovery and dealing with negative emotions, either making it or breaking it. If you don't use it, you lose it. Sharing techniques and formulas that have helped me stay on recovery and not lose focus of what I do know. Now, I choose to share this with you.

I did not spend thousands of dollars in recovery. I used simple techniques and formulas that have been helpful to and for me. Bottom line is these techniques kept me on the path to recovery from the days of blow until the present. This is not just your ordinary recovery book. This is from someone who has been there and survived... MIRACULOUSLY.

IF I CAN DO IT. YOU CAN DO IT TOO!

# I

# TED DEMME

## Death of a filmmaker

### JAN 13, 2002

Kristina and I had made plans after the new year to have a family and friends get-together brunch on Sunday Jan. 13, 2002. Following our meal, we decided to watch a movie together.

As the T.V. was turned on and while everyone was finding a place to sit, we saw something scrolling on the ticker at the bottom of the screen that shocked us all. While still in my seat, and still rattled by what I had just read on the TV screen...

The phone rings, looking at the caller ID it's Ted Demme's assistant Emma, her number is being displayed on the small monitor. Answering the call Emma says "Mirtha Teddy's in the hospital. I will keep you posted, things do not look good."

As I slowly hung up the phone, I was looking over in the direction of Kristina and Darla. They could tell by the expression on my face that something serious or terrible had occurred. Over and over in my head I just kept remembering the time...

All I could think of was the night in the beginning of the project Blow, driving around in Los Angeles, trying to find a place to eat. As most places of the places were busy, we moved on to the next place. Reminiscing of that night with Teddy. The director of the movie Blow was dead.

Talking with him about the making of the movie is when I first expressed my fears. I was scared that someone would die during production. He smiled and shrugged it off as if not worried about it. We were in his SUV that night and we almost got hit by another vehicle.

Racing through my mind, like a movie. I went to the bathroom to splash water on my face, as I stood over the sink with my eyes closed, I heard Teddy's voice telling me "It's going to be alright, it's going to be alright", I heard his voice ringing clearly in my ears and it brought a sense of complete calmness. I was overcome by a strange inner peace. I felt his reassurance. I believed everything was going to be all right. I knew without a doubt that his spirit had come to visit me, that there was indeed another side.

I had gotten to know Teddy off the set. We would sit for hours talking about George, life, and adventures. Teddy had a child-like quality about him, he was much younger than I had expected.

His understanding of fatherhood, how important it was to be a good father, and always taking responsibility as we kept talking and sharing ideas. Being a good father himself. He always made me laugh by doing imitations of movie characters. One of his favorites to do was the Blue's Brothers. It had taken 6 years to get to this point in our relationship.

He treated me with kindness, he was charming but also serious when he needed to be. My feelings were important to him and that of the family. It had been a very long time since anyone had been that considerate towards me. My life had really changed from the days of doing cocaine.

Teddy was very much impressed by the fact that I had taken control of my life and went clean & sober for years. These memories were flooding my mind.

I returned to the living room. I told Kristina and the others that I just heard his voice telling me it was going to be all right, they too were amazed by what I said, but they understood exactly what I meant.

Once again, the phone rang, I got up to answer the call, it was Emma calling back. Her voice filled with sadness, she said, "Teddy is gone Mirtha. I will get back to you with the information, date, time, and hotel so you can attend the memorial. I feel so overwhelmed Mirtha! Let's talk later, I have so much to take care of," after that she hung up…

A wave of total devastation came over me. Washing away all the plans and ideas we had dreamed of. He assured me that he would be there for me as long as he was alive.

We could not believe it. Nine months after the release of Blow, again appearing at the bottom of the television screen the crawler was being viewed again, it said filmmaker Ted Demme dies at 38 years old, last movie directed Blow.

I began to feel a deep sadness, I started to think to myself of his newborn son and his daughter having to live a life without their father. Wondering how his wife was holding up? Knowing his son would never get to know him in the physical being. Neither one of the children would ever feel his love and warmth.

We were all talking about our trip to Hollywood. Penelope Cruz had a lot of characteristics that reminded me of myself. There had been talk about Jennifer Lopez for the role, however I was surprised when I was told Penelope had accepted the role. We talked about the memories we shared while we were there working along with him on the production of the movie Blow.

Teddy and I had made plans for my 50th birthday and who I wanted to meet. It was funny to me. I would run the list of stars' names by him. As I would mention a few names to him, he would stop and say, "That's a problem! We'll see." Other stars' names he would say "Yup, no problem." It would make me laugh.

He felt Penelope was the right character for the role, I had to admit, she was. Although I didn't have an accent as she did, she did fit the role. Never the less, he was the director of the movie, the Boss. Remembering the arrangement, he made for me to meet Johnny Depp at his home as a birthday present. How awesome was that? Here I was meeting Johnny Depp.

Making reservations at the Four Seasons Hotel on Doheny drive in Beverly Hills. Arrangements for an exclusive V.I.P. dinner party were made. Feeling like a VIP, I was.

Attending dinner was Joel Stillerman and other exec-producers along with Paul Rubens. I was dressed in a black jumpsuit made of crepe material. Thinking of all this that had happened. Teddy's dream was to be nominated for his film Blow. Always calling it his baby. Oscar for his outstanding performance in the scene when Johnny bangs on the plexiglass with the phone in his hand. Therefore, he told me "You should know, that scene never happened in real life. I never visited George in jail."

The government would not allow it.

Seventeen scripts it took to finally come up with the one. In between the chaos, the other writers were caught up in writing other movies. Blow was behind schedule. Teddy decides to write it. Turning it into a comedy. Johnny got to the point that he told Teddy that when the script was final he would then read it. For it, was all changing again and repeatedly rewriting the script? Just like this book.

It was exciting to sit next to Teddy. Learning and watching the process of a motion picture being filmed, bringing characters to life. It was bigger than life. I had never known the true meaning of what it was like until I had the experienced being on the set. The Silver Screen, the big screen. It was so interesting to see Johnny and the other actors and actresses watching how it was being filmed, their body language, the characters with their script, each one remembering his or her lines without help. Not having to look at the script. Learning about the timing of each shot. Smoke that comes up from the floor, everything done in rhythm. The days were long and when he said action it was completely quiet on the set. It was deathly quiet. Short breaks were taken. Start early in the morning with the makeup artist, you really come to understand their great acting ability. Johnny Depp and extras being positioned in whatever scene they are called to do. There was a cameo of Teddy in the movie. Teddy is the lawyer that goes to visit George with the tape recorder, so he can record his last words to his father before he dies.

How it all came about was George's father Fred was gravely ill. I needed and wanted George to know. I called his lawyer letting him know Fred was running out of time. Fred had not fully recuperated from his cancer and now it was catching up with him. I had kept in touch with Fred and Ermine, they were good grandparents to Kristina. They always made sure to talk to their granddaughter Kristina and always sending her things through the years.

Reminiscing about what we had talked about as far as the movie and how great it was going to be. His baby, as he called it. We continued to channel surf as to catch any additional information on his status. Reality was settling in. Day in and day out, wanting to hear from Emma, not wanting to call her because I knew she would call confirming his passing. It had come painfully true. Full circle, he was gone.

Emma calls again, we continued to talk for a bit, it was the first funeral that she had ever planned. It was overwhelming for her. Especially making these types of arrangements, calling his friends and having to stay strong for Teddy's family. For she was his assistant, a young, lovely woman, resembling a much younger Uma Thurman. Waiting for the death certificate of the deceased to be signed, no one had expected this. Ted's wife Amanda lost in sorrow and pain over the death of her husband. Having their first-born son Dexter who was only a few weeks old. All so sad. Death in different stages.

Finally, Emma called with the details for the memorial. Grabbing a pen and writing down the information, I told her I would call her as soon as we got there. It was amazing that the next time I would meet with him would be to say my final good-bye at his memorial. Rumors were out that an autopsy would be done to test him for coke in the hopes that the rumors would be put to rest. Being that he had directed the movie Blow about cocaine, there was speculation about his cocaine use.

We started packing and beginning our journey to L.A to pay our respects to Ted. Kristina and her baby were with us, so it made the ride longer having to make several stops along the way. Finally getting to our hotel and checking in. It was nice. We unpacked and started to get ready for the big event. Only difference, it was not a movie in production, it was the finale for Teddy and all the dreams we both shared. All vanished now. The dreams, his friendship, and financial ruin. It was devastating.

Still in the back of my mind, I could hear him say it's going to be all right. We got ready and headed towards the location for the memorial. Upon arriving, we had to go through security, huge signs posted everywhere, no cameras, no recorders. I had never seen so many stars gather all in one place. They were there to pay their respects to Teddy. Danny DeVito and his wife. Paul Rubens took me over to them and introduced us. All these famous people, Carmen Diaz, Michael Fox, Dennis Leary, and Leonardo DiCaprio.

We waited in line just as everyone else did. Then we started to move and enter the tent. It was a beautiful giant white tent. All these candles burning. The glow of the candles radiated this beautiful spiritual mood. The memorial started, the first opening lines being spoken were... "It is going to be all right." With it being said more than once, it was at that moment I knew without a doubt that he had come to visit me that day.

The memorial ended, it followed with a reception later that day. Everyone started to depart. I was able to see Amanda and give her a hug. In reply, she whispered in my ear how glad she felt to see me there. She looked so sad, and you could see it and feel it in her eyes. Lost in the pain of losing Ted, so unexpectedly.

We attended the reception and once again there were more stars. The ones that could not attend the memorial service earlier were there now. Toasting and giving him credit for his endeavors in the movie industry and music. He had gotten to meet Bob Dylan and that was a big thing, for Bob Dylan did not just go to any screening of a production, let alone do a song for the movie, which was the music you hear when I give birth to Kristina. Bob Dylan was Georges idol. Later we learned that Johnny Depp knew Bob Dylan. He was so excited and thanked me, for if it had not been for the movie Blow, he would have never gotten to meet him.

Going into the details of when Bob Dylan arrived, in his voice, you could hear the excitement filling the sparkle in his eyes. As he laughed, saying that everybody was in the front of the building waiting for Dylan and here was Dylan coming in the back, so those that were in the front missed him. As he came in, Dylan was with five blonde-haired women to see the first premiere of the movie Blow. Repeatedly all he could say was how great it was to meet Bob Dylan.

All of this was going through my mind. Sitting there at the reception. Leary and Nick had also toasted to George as he looked at me, he knew exactly by the look in my eyes. I was sad, after all George could not be there once again missing out. Thinking how nice it was for him to toast George. It was amazing that all the stars had attended.

Ted Demme was 38 years old. Nine months after the release of Blow, on 9/11, the DVD video of Blow was to be released that day. World Trade Center gets bombed. Early morning, recalling the phone call, it was Teddy saying, "Turn on the TV quickly Mirtha, look what's happening in New York City!" I could see one of the towers crumbling, I couldn't believe my eyes, here it's supposed to be an exciting day for the DVDs and video and here we were watching the World Trade Center under attack by a plane.

Sharing his feelings with me about when his father and mother were planning separation and what a shock it was to him. He had just returned from college that year when his parents gave him the news. It made him stronger, at the same time, he was crushed, knowing his parents were getting a divorce.

His uncle Jonathan Demme who won numerous Academy Awards for Silence of the Lambs. Also, directing Beloved with Oprah Winfrey. Teddy wanted to be his own person, he did not want to be compared to his uncle Jonathan Demme.

The movie Blow was nominated for a Crystal Ball Award.

We miss you dearly Teddy.

Mirtha with Paul Ruebens at Blow Premier

Teddy On Set

Teddy Here's Looking At You Kid

Teddy and Mirtha

The Two Mirtha's

# II

❊

# ROOTS

## Planted and Transplanted

E arly 1950's throughout the island, the wind blowing a whisper of a man called Fidel Castro. Cuba being 90 miles off the coast of Florida, USA. There was a feeling of insecurity among the men in our family and their conversations were about that it might be a good idea to go to the embassy and start the legal paper work for migration to the U.S. Having their papers all in order was a priority, thinking they might have to travel.

As the days unfolded, the planning of migrating to the USA was becoming real. Interviews back and forth at the embassy, it was becoming apparent that they had to be ready in the event they made the choice to leave Cuba. This was on their minds, also leaving behind their country, tradition, and culture.

It had started to make them think of how sad and bad it might get or could get. There were a lot of signs it was not going to get better. Then after their last visit to the embassy, they all had their papers. Authorization to leave, their precious lives, and the only country they had known.

It was getting bad and they were living in fear, so they started to make plane ticket reservations and packed what they could. As they packed and cried they would tell their friends in a short time they were leaving the country. Time and confirmation of their flight came, and they now had a date and time to leave. They were packed and driving to the airport to catch their flight. Boarding their flight, the plane taking off, above in the clouds they looked down feeling a sadness of leaving everything behind but as they flew they knew they were transplanting themselves to a foreign soil that was so rich.

The country of opportunity and freedom, thinking to themselves someday they would return. In a short-time they were in Florida, U.S.A.

Landing in FLA and going through customs, on the way to catch one more flight. A flight that would take them to the Midwest, destination, Chicago Illinois. The windy city. The readiness to tackle the cold with their coats was exciting for them. Snow so impressive for they had never seen it before in life. Not really thinking of how cold it would actually be arriving in winter.

It was very cold. Nevertheless, the excitement and jet lag gave no room for thought. Being with their beloved family and wanting to reunite with them made it all worth the bearing the cold.

As their plane landed, their sisters, and brother in laws were waiting. Waiting to see them, my mom waving and coming their way, embracing, kissing and hugging full of excitement and joy. A gladness to see each other and once again being together finally, all of them as a family. A huge relief knowing that they were out of danger.

They all had transplanted to the new world and they were happy. Days went by and they started to settle in different areas of Chicago. When we first arrived, we settled in the South area, and then soon thereafter moved to the north area of Chicago. Jobs in factories were available, and even if it was hard work, they knew it was the only way to live as residents. The English language was not necessary when working in a factory or on the assembly line. It was mostly labor-intensive work. After a few months the realization started to set in. How far away it was to buy the products and foods accustomed to them. Café Bustelo had our traditional espresso that we drank often. Even though it was far they knew where it was sold and the availability of other products they used and needed as well.

We went to church as a family every Sunday. We were being educated in a private catholic school. It was very costly for working class people. Every month the tuition had to be paid. Sundays were our fun day. The family would take turns as to who would host each Sunday gathering. Rotating my grandmother was always a part of any functions.

Sitting around the dinner table, understanding that whoever sat at the head of the table at dinner would recite the prayer. Enjoying each other's company. Prayer would always be about how blessed we were, and grateful to be in America.

After dinner, they would gather around the old radio and listen to the broadcasts coming out of Havana. It was getting worse for the Cuban people there. Fidel Castro was gaining control of the country.

During the summers, they would plan family reunions. Allowed to have activities such as bowling, swimming, along with music classes and during the winters it was ice-skating. Adjusting to the American culture. Family picnics at the lake. We would head to Indiana, there was a spot they liked and got used to visiting. It was always a fun ride there and back.

As for our cousins and siblings they were getting married starting families of their own even while being so young themselves. Having to get married for they knew nothing about protection and how innocent they were. Everyone was getting older and adjusting. Knowing how to get around the city easier, along with the language becoming easier for them to understand. There were few Spanish people back then too. The Puerto Ricans where around, but mostly scattered here and there.

The word Latino was not used. Politically correct did not even exist. You were Spanish.

Ambition in there being and fire in their blood, working hard is what they did. Therefore, we never had to do without. A new system of freedom, voting, and taxes. The dinners and the activities continue, as well as going to church. We had a daily routine and then on weekends they were grateful and devoted Catholics. Sounded like a stable American family back in the days. Not exactly, as in Leave it to Beaver, or Dennis the menace. Boxing on Saturdays was great entertainment and once again, we always gathered with my grandmother to watch the boxing matches. We had gone from radio to TV in black and white. Then it came, the news they were all fearing. Castro had taken over Cuba and it was out of hand. Friends were contacting them asking for help to flee Cuba and come to the USA and they helped.

Thinking how they had been blessed. Making the decision way before Fidel had taken over Cuba. Leaving their roots, they were grateful to have made the right decision.

It was all coming together for them. Some of us in college and me feeling different along with my cousin William. Mastering the English language. It made them proud for us to excel in school.

Our family had started to integrate with white American Anglo Saxons, little knowledge did they have of Pilgrims or Pioneers. For us it was history. American History. Sharing with them gave them knowledge. As the years passed, we became more Americanized. We were changing, and it was unacceptable to them. As foreigners, our traditions, cultures, and even our language was being changed by their children.

1971 is the death of my cousin William. Being a good soul, he was very down to earth. He wanted to be a lead singer in a band. The family was outraged with my aunt Tia, for they believed it was too much freedom for William. Letting his hair grow long, they thought something could happen to him. It did as the war ended. Other family members were coming back from Vietnam.

The USA was changing. Protesting, smoking weed, and taking L.S.D. seemed to be popular with everyone. Calling it a trip. Yes, a hallucination drug that lasted at least 10 hours. It was a powerful drug and said it had been put out by the government by mistake, it was to open your mind. According to the government it was believed to be like a truth serum, it was amazing, the total transformation the country was taking.

Blacks walking down the street and no longer riding in the back of the bus. Chanting as they marched for freedom and equality. A man known as Martin Luther King leading them in their march. It did change at home for us too. Our parents did not want us to speak English and we only spoke Spanish as it was demanded of us.

We had respect for our elders and our parents. They were strict.

The 50's had come and gone, along with the 60's, and into the 70's now. I had been married and divorced once already. More and more black and white couples were getting together. Racial integration. Everywhere there was this energy and the choice of drugs was expanding. Songs left, right, and then boom disco hits. As we had become older so had the family, me being the first to file for divorce in my family.

We were the younger generation. Therefore, it was a good start. We were to leave Chicago after my grandmother died, it was for the best, for my cousin William had passed too. Life had changed, and it was time we made a change too. The realization had come to focus. There was no reason for us to ever return to Cuba. Friends and relatives had transplanted to the U.S.A. permanently. The dream that was close to their hearts of returning to Cuba had died.

The action all starts after my sister Martha decides to leave Chicago and moves to New York. She is now doing well and has met this wonderful and caring man. He is Columbian, and they have fallen in love with each other. Love birds tweeting. When she spoke to our mother there was excitement, for she was coming to visit us. Once she arrived, she spoke with and made plans with our mother to go. Mother was game and so was I. Martha wanted for all of us to come to New York with her, that would fulfill her dream.

Our mother realizing there was no longer any reason for us to stay in Chicago, nor return to Cuba, chose to follow my sister to New York. The dream my mother once held dearly, the dream of one day going back to the homeland, Mi Tierra, had been whisked away. My grandmother had just passed away, so it made the decision easier for her. A month of planning, packing, and saying our goodbyes to relatives. We were ready to move. As soon as the school year ended, we were gone.

New York City! Here we come.

Arriving in Florida

Clara's 1st Birthday

Family on airport steps

Mirtha and family arriving in USA from Cuba

Mirtha's 9th birthday party

Mirtha's birthday

Mirtha's 1st Holy Communion

Mirtha, William and Mama

Mirtha, Grandma and ex-brother in law

# III

# EAST COAST
## N.Y., Mass, Fl.

L iving through the 70's and 80's was like flying on a magic carpet. Although it was hard to leave once again, with everything we had been accustomed to, we saw it as a positive step. We all saw it as a change that would lead us to a new and better life.

New York was an exciting city that was full of culture. There was lots of change that came along with the new life. My parents were getting up in age. Willie, my sister's husband, wanted her to be happy. Her three children, her mother, stepfather Papa John, myself and my daughter. This was the immediate family.

A huge responsibility for any man. William was a banker in his country of Columbia. He had made some great investments.

As he was very much in love with her, he always wanted to please her. The impression we got of him was that of a very caring man and with impeccable manners.

My mother thought it was wonderful that Willie was willing to take care and provide for her and the family. It made life easier for all of us. We were happy. Willie got us a place to move into at 72nd and Central Park.

Within months life started to change for the better. Flats were hard to find unless you knew the Super, also known as the manager, in different areas of the country. Nothing was hard to get in New York City. If you couldn't buy it, you had it manufactured. Soon thereafter, we moved to a corner flat along the Hudson Parkway. The entrance to our place was out of the elevator leading into a foyer. The flat was huge! The windows faced the Hudson River. When you turned your head to the right, this specular view of the George Washington Bridge could be seen. A bedroom for each of us, huge living room, huge dining room, amazing kitchen, with lots of cabinets and shelves. We were so excited. It was comfortable. It even came with a security guard as you entered the building. We were so happy to be living in this new place, everything was going right, everyone was happy and completely enjoying where we lived. Looking back and knowing it was a good move.

Taking you back now 10 years. Early 70's. This is how it really starts. The relationship had been well-established years before when Yamel and my sister Martha married into the family. Yamel's biological father was married twice. The first marriage was to Merced, had a son named Juan, which made Yamel the half-sister to Juan. Juan and my sister Martha married and later had a girl.

Juan being an entertainer, was working nights in clubs. He was a fantastic piano player. He had plenty of gigs, it was his only source of income. Nevertheless, it started to take a toll on the marriage. The biological mother was very possessive of her son. There was additional hurt to the marriage and soon they started to fall and tumble. An agreement was made. They would get a divorce, for that was the only option.

There was a strong bond between my sister Martha, and Yamel. Martha knew and was very close with Yamel's mother also. This is how she meets William. Yamel introduces Willie to her and they fall in love. This is how it all starts. The rise to the Cartels. Little did you know, it was, for us, *all in the family.*

When I arrive in New York, I am introduced to Yamel and right away we hit it off. My sister thought it was a good idea for both of us to hang out together. At the time, I had a great job on Fifth Avenue.

Yamel and I got along great. It was a brand-new life. Disco was up and coming. These exclusively-private clubs coming up on the horizon. It was a very different crowd with money, all doing great enough to be impressive to me at 21 years old. Nevertheless, I had a child. I was young and starting all over again with my first daughter Clara, so living with my parents was ideal.

Being with Yamel, while getting to know her and some of her hangouts, some were nice, and some were horrid. She kept different crowds. From low to high just as the drugs she did, I still had no idea about the coke yet.

Yamel asked if I wanted to go to a private club. I had never been to one, so I agreed and off we went. As we drove in her black beamer pulling up to this storefront place I thought to myself, "what kind of club this could be?", via the looks of it.

Riding around in the beamer that night, we would go to this club where she knew these friends of Diego. There was talk that he was getting out of prison soon. It was during this time George and Diego start to mastermind the game. I had not put it together yet at this time, for I did not even know George yet. Diego and George are getting to know each other being in Danbury, Connecticut, as they both were sharing a cell together.

We got out and went through the front doors. There was a man standing in front of the elevators at the end of the hall. He greeted us as we walked towards him. Yamel was known and needed no password. The man entered the elevator, telling us to come with him. He pressed the number 2 on the elevator panel, and we stood in silence as the elevator began to move slowly. When we arrived at the 2nd floor, he led us through another set of doors that brought us into an enormous and beautifully decorated room with a wall-to-wall salt-water fish tank. The man then said to Yamel that Al was waiting to see her, then he turned around and left.

Yamel knew her way around the place. Looking at me she said, "Come, follow me.". As I followed her from room to room, it was different than anything I had ever seen. A game room, rooms broken off into sections with one side a pool table and, on the other side a card room. A dance room with a round disco ball. It was, to say the least, a fit for whatever mood you were in. There was a full bar with the finest liquors you could drink, complete with midnight snacks. A different setting throughout the each of the rooms, it was a maze. Finally, a door that had the words PRIVATE DO NOT ENTER written in bold black letters. Yamel knocks. A handsome young man opens the door. Walking in as though she owed the place, Al got up and gave her a kiss and a hug. Yamel introduced me to this well-dressed man about twenty- three years old from South America.

I meet Cesar. We started talking, we danced, and later that evening we exchanged beeper numbers. Afterward, we started to see each other on regular basis. He wanted to meet my parents and my daughter Claire. We set a date and time and he came over for dinner to meet my daughter and parents. My parents and Claire all fell in love with him. It was that evening he asked me to marry him. A beautiful emerald with diamonds. He asked my parents for their blessing.

Great young man my dad thought. "Another Columbian", my mom said. After all, this was New York City. Liking the fact that he liked Claire was another plus factor for him. He had never been married, nor did he have any children. He was from a good family, and my mom just loved him.

It made things much easier. Being thoughtful of my daughter and always making sure she got special attention from him. As the months passed we started to make plans to marry on his parent's estate. A huge wedding in Columbia.

He would go in and out of the country. In addition, he was friends with Diego and Yamel. He knew Diego, but they did not run in the same circle of friends. His friends were like the club owner, Al. I liked Cesar and we had fun. He would be gone for a few weeks and then return to the states. Living at home and going to school, partying became less and less. Waiting for Cesar to return to the states, we did family things, even though I knew within myself I was not in love with him. My parents were pleased, and my daughter loved him. My sister and her husband liked him too.

Family was happy, especially knowing we were engaged, but I felt trapped. As time went on, Yamel started to talk more and more about Diego. He would soon be joining her, as she explained, they would get married. Diego had been arrested and busted for car theft. He was exporting the cars to Columbia for good money. Stupid things young people do. In the back of my mind I wanted to meet an American guy. I would ask her,

"Don't you know any American guys?". She knew none. It was amazing to think, she knew none. Yamel was becoming excited that her man was coming home, after all, he was her first. There was a huge celebration planned for Diego, a welcome home party.

Finally, Yamel and Diego arrived at the party.

A toast to their reunion. Diego was a handsome man. I had only seen pictures of him. While at the gathering, he laughed at his own stories about his crime. Being a car thief was over for him. Calling it a petty crime. So, this was Diego? A thief. A criminal. After he got out, Diego and Yamel became less available. I saw her less and less. Both flying back and forth from Columbia. Diego being Columbian, and his mother living there. Little did I know what was really going on.

This is how George and I really meet. Not at a wedding as seen in the movie.

Although he was in the bridal party. He was the best man at Diego and Yamel's wedding. It was a very private ceremony. George and I really meet at the hotel in New York City. The hotel is where we met.

My sister needed to go to the Hilton at LaGuardia airport. There was a man waiting to see Willie, her husband. The man was a business associate, El Americano. Being that she was pregnant, she wanted me to drive her, she did not want to go alone. I really didn't want to, but I felt bad, especially in her pregnant condition. So, I agreed to take her. There we were, taking the drive to the *edge of darkness*.

It seemed so innocent when I look back... Willie was sick since the night before. Another reason for me to take her. My sister, with her soft-spoken words, always got what she wanted. We were close and being her sister, I always felt love from her.

Even though years have passed, her love has always remained the same for me.

On the way there she talked about this place that her and Willie had just bought. A place in the Palisades, a very nice area in New York. They would be moving there after the baby was born, anting me to see the new place as well.

We pull up to the Hilton. Finding a parking space, she insists that I go with her. It was going to take a while and she did not want me waiting in the parking lot.

Once again, there I was agreeing with her, going along. Got to the lobby and took the elevator. I was going up in the elevator, so she could meet with this man. Georgie! El Americano.

We get to the floor and approach his room number. We stop, she knocks on the door, and the door opens. We're greeted by this white woman who lets us in, then we wait in the living room. It was a suite. She comes back and asks that we follow her to the room where he is waiting. She leaves us in the room with him. He was an American. A handsome older guy, around my sister's age. We looked at each other briefly. I was young and still naïve. I had not put it together yet. This was the first time I had gotten close to the truth of the real story. Still not knowing all the under layers. Not even an idea or a hint. Nor a clue. He was special to Willie and my sister. **Hmmmm...**

He asked my sister, "Who is this beautiful woman Martha?". My sister laughed knowing what was in the back of his mind. Her reply was "She is my sister and soon to be married with Cesar, you know the coffee heir from Columbia." George knew who he was, but it did not stop him from being the charming man that he was. Those hazel eyes so dazzlingly, along with his blonde hair, made an attractive combination. He was tall and lean, but above all, he was educated. A total eloquent look. We exchange this look and my sister caught it. "Georgie!", she said.

Just then, Martha asked me to go into the other room. Without question, I did. I was looking through the magazines he had lying out. He had a Time Magazine, this was interesting to me. Now I look back and know why he had the magazine. It was to stay up with the news of the drug trade and how the government was handling the situation.

My sister walks into the room and says to me, "Time to go." She clearly does not care for his flirty ways towards me and becomes serious in her good-bye. On the way back, I was asking her questions about him, but her reply was she was tired and not feeling well. She needed to nap the rest of the way back. I left it at that. The next day there is a person at the front door. It's the Americano. I didn't know he was coming. Willie was waiting for him.

He comes in and I look at him with wonder. Being he was the first and only Americano to visit the flat where we lived. I found this to be strange but at the same time, I was happy to see him.

There was this attraction, and thus the confusion starts for me. We hit it off. I was taken by him, but still not knowing what exactly his connection to Willie and was. Only that they were in business. Being 21 years old, I was captivated by his manners and his accent. He was from Massachusetts. I had been there much earlier in life, there was so much history there. Another plus factor.

I found myself playing the piano for him. He was impressed as we chatted and laughed. Meanwhile, Willy was getting upset, as well as throwing up. He wanted the Americano to leave.

As far as Willie was concerned, the only business they had was cocaine. George, being the connection to the west coast. It was their fear, I think, of us getting together.

This is how he gets into the family. This is how it happens. The flat was quiet that evening, for my father had just passed away. We stayed up through the night into the early hours of the morning together, until we decided to run out and get a bite to eat. Getting back to the flat and now the Americano George was going back to Boston. During this time, he is telling me how he believes in love at first sight. Listening to his refined words and large vocabulary were very enchanting. Giving me his parent's phone number, we had made plans to talk on specific dates and times. He was into precious metals at the time, it would be hard to call again if I missed his call. No one, but my mother, knew that we were talking to each other.

He is off to Boston. I must face William. I remember getting there. William was outraged, he wanted all the details. He wanted to know where we had been and what we had done. "Scandalous", he said. This was scandalous.

Days passed. Knowing I had to call Cesar and break the news to him, the wedding was off. Not being able to tell him, I had met someone else. Repeatedly, his voice would go from high to low. "Why? What happened?". My father passing away was another major factor, but not enough reason to leave him with all the wedding preparations and all the invitations to the all their guests in Columbia, already sent with date and time.

Now, George and I talking three to four times a day. I found myself waiting for his calls. The phone would ring, and it was George, always on time. I was making plans to meet him in Boston and go away with him to the Bahamas.

It did not matter at this point, for the conversations we shared were about getting together and being happy. We had broken all the rules.

My mother knew, for I confided in her with everything. She was happy for me, but at the same time upset knowing how this was not going to settle well between my sister and her husband. Not knowing what to think for she knew there was Caesar and a wedding planned in Columbia.

We went shopping and she could feel and see how happy I truly was. Helping me pick out my wardrobe to wear on my trip to meet up with George. I left for Boston. So, there I am at Logan airport where he is waiting to pick me up and to take us to a room at the Logan Hilton Hotel.

"We will wait there," as he is saying all of this in the limo complete with roses and champagne. We celebrated our reunion on the way there. I was surprised. I am thinking that we were just going to meet there and catch the next flight to Miami, then the Bahamas. He has other plans.

Arriving and checking into the Hilton, we go to the room. Opening the door, the aroma of roses filled the air. Settling in, he is telling me how he has fallen in love. "I cannot wait for us to be together". He calls room service and orders us a bottle of champagne. We toasted to love and being together. He tells me he must go and take care of business. We kiss and embrace. He will return as soon as possible and to be patient and wait.

It seemed hours before he came back to the hotel. When he returned, it seemed he was disturbed about something. I asked, and his reply was, "Its nothing". I felt there was more to the story, but I did not press the issue. I felt in due time he would tell me. Excited and in love, I was happy for the first time in my life.

We checked out and headed to the airport, then caught our flight to Miami to make our connection to the Bahamas. Both of us were happy. I was not aware he was to meet with Diego and Yamel. He had to call Yamel and Diego letting them know we were on our way. Boarding our flight, taking our seats, and then taking off. While in flight we were talking and planning to live in Massachusetts. His mom and dad lived there during this time. He was happy. He had not felt this happy since before Linda had died, his late girlfriend.

I didn't know we were going to meet Diego and Yamel. I thought it was strange that Diego and Yamel would be in the Bahamas. After all Diego and George were friends, and here I am coming with him unexpectedly. Yamel had no idea I had met him. On the way there, he tells me that the business he was taking care of was breaking it off with Betsy, his now, ex-girlfriend. I was in disbelief, but I didn't care, for he was with me. I should have known better looking back.

We land in the Bahamas, limo waiting to take us to the hotel. Diego knew he was waiting for him at the hotel and not at all disturbed that he has met me and is with me. It was a big surprise to Yamel. She was outraged that the big surprise George had, was in fact, Mirtha.

Wanting to know how he had met me and bad mouthing me to him, telling him not to trust me. It was intense dislike. I was shocked at her reaction to me being with him. We spent a week there, then went back to Florida to meet up again with Diego and Yamel. This time at the Castaways.

We arrived at the Castaways. I started to tell George that Yamel and Diego had a huge problem in New York, it was pending resolution once they got there. There was a hit was put on them. Some people needed to take up business with them. I was not sure, but I was certain it was not good.

George confided in Diego about the trap set for them in New York. George saved their lives that night.

George makes his plan to catch the red eye to California, so he can meet up with Derek, Dennis, and Scott, only to find out that Diego had already gotten there. Derek unknowingly gave George's money to Diego. It was Georges cut of the previous deal. Over a million dollars.

Derek's explanation was, "George, he said you wanted him to pick it up for you. Being that you trust him like a brother, I gave it to him."

It was at that point George realizes the betrayal and foul play. Camelot and the Knight of the Roundtable... betrayed and hurt, it was painful knowing what Diego had done to him.

Now George is calling me at the hotel and telling me what just happened. I am amazed. He needs money to fly back to Florida, so I pay for the plane fare for him to return to Florida. This is where it really starts to take place. We have only been together two weeks and already the negative forces are preparing themselves for the takeover.

George had no money at this point, the only money he had was what his father was hanging onto for him. He needed to make plans for us to go back to Boston. We jumped on the plane and flew to Boston. Not knowing I would be stopping at his parent's house and spending a few days there. I got to know them. Once again, he tells me he must take care of business, leaving me there with his parents. Meanwhile, I am calling my mom and sister telling them what has happened and asking about my daughter Claire. Both listening intensely to what has happened between Diego and him. Diego had gotten him good.

The other side of the story now.

Since we had gone to Massachusetts, we needed to establish a place. Within a week, we were living in Eastham, Massachusetts. A beautiful house on the beach, it was paradise.

We started to settle in Eastham around his friends and people who worked for him, life was grand. Just George and me. Flying back and forth to see Claire for she was still in school. I was happy despite what had happened. I was in paradise.

Making it into a home. Meanwhile, back in New York the Colombians were outraged.

My sister and my mom wanted me to be happy, but it was upsetting to them. Especially for her husband, for it had all happened in less than six months of my arrival to New York.

A scandal leaving Caesar at the altar with everything already purchased. The wedding dress, the whole 9 yards, this was scandalous indeed. I didn't really care how they felt or thought, because I knew it was the real thing between George and me. We had nick names, mine was **Birdie** and his was **Tobacco.**

Living together had started for us on the cape. With the money he had put away, he could buy time to think of the situation with Diego. Diego was no longer in one place, he had taken over transportation. He was moving around was the news that was out. He was becoming very rich and powerful, as my sister would always tell me what was being said.

Diego had taken transportation to another level. He was already buying an island to be able to refuel without having to stop in the Bahamas. The news started to take a toll on George.

George and I got along great and we had intellectual conversation. His political views, his joys, and happiness surrounded us. As he said in the movie, "We had it all." As the week passed, it was taking a toll on him. I mentioned to him, "Why did you tell Diego about the hit? They were waiting for them in New York." I had confided in him, this was another problem between him and the Colombians. He said he loved Diego and he was his brother. He trusted him.

Weeks passed, and school was getting out soon for Claire. I could now afford to give her the best of everything money could buy. Here we are, and it is all coming together for us.

Cigars, cognac, lobster, and all the coke and pot you could consume. Along with money in a 5-drawer chest. He would stack up the hundred-dollar bills he had. I would take a few bundles and head to the mall. This beautiful house had rooms downstairs, intercoms, and eventually we would have servants with their own living quarters. Sharing my life with him. Anytime his knights came over, no one wanted to leave, for he always had an army around him. He was the Boss. The King. Was he really?

Our house was starting to feel like a home. Claire's room being decorated according to her age, hoping she would be happy too. She was now 8 years old. A custom dollhouse being made, complete with furniture. George wanted Claire to like him. He was concerned with her being happy too.

Things had changed for George. Diego was becoming very powerful. Buying planes, cars, homes and building an army of his own. The Colombian Medellin Cartel was rising.

The day is coming, and it was time to pick Claire up. As the plane landed and taxied in, George and I are overwhelmingly excited. As the passengers started to come down the gate looking for her, I see her, and she comes running to us. Picking her up, hugging, and kissing her. We could not wait to get back to the house. Anxious for her to see her own room and all the presents we had for her. It was one of the happiest days of my life. Finally, I could give her all the things a mother could hope for. To see her face light up when she opened her bedroom to notice she had a swing in her room. I will never forget that day. Being a family was all I wanted. As the weeks passed, we were adjusting, and we had the privacy. George had stopped having people over. We started to become a family. Family dinners, going shopping to buy clothes, a dog, a piano, fish tank. Happy to see the smile on Claire's face from the deck, watching her walk along the beach shore. A great feeling of security and peace.

Little did I know about the coke addition and what would happen later in life.

George was wanting to have a party. We decided together to have a celebration for the 4$^{th}$ of July. Making a list of those that we would invite. The VIP's, the Colombians. The Cartel.

As we started to plan for this big event, George looked at the fourth as a true Americano. A great day for America. Colombians really had no idea, except for that it was a holiday. What they knew was fear of being blown up, for the blow. La coca. Like firecrackers.

It was our first family party. A few months had passed after my cancelling of the wedding to Cesar. The family knew it was beyond their control. One by one, they accepted the invitation and rsvp'd to come and stay at casa El Americano.

As we sat and decided on the menu, it was simple and tasteful. George wanted champagne and grilled lobster, along with finest catering chef and it was done. It was going to be an event. It was exciting for him, now they were coming. It was the best way to handle the situation with Diego. That was the real motive as I look back. Still upset about the broken engagement to Cesar, it did not matter now. The Medellin Cartel had money, power, and George. Oh, and then there was yours truly. Family togetherness. After all, he was now married into the family.

As the Fourth of July approached it was exciting knowing that soon the house would be rocking.

The Colombians showing up on time as they always did, dressed in relaxed linen attire, dark sunglasses, guns, and bodyguards. Together at last and toasting to health. They were not impressed with the location of the house. Talking among themselves, they were saying how it was unsafe. It was no place to live, it was too dangerous, and you could end up disappearing.

Their feeling of paranoia was setting in. Blow wasn't even being sorted snorted at the time. George knew... I was translating everything they were saying to him. He could not believe it and started to get upset. He was calling them names and telling them how crazy they were. He was right.

George taking a small vial from his pocket, the Colombians wondering what he is doing. It was getting around that George was becoming an addict to his own product and this was not good at all. Mister Georgie snorting coke in front of their eyes. This was disrespectful, especially to William, my sisters' husband. He was against anyone snorting it, and especially doing it in front of other family members. William was outraged at seeing this. Especially when business was still to be conducted. It was always business, as usual for them.

Within a few hours at the house, they were all ready to leave. The fear overcame them, it was the isolation of a place that was totally unknown to them. It was much too isolated for them. Feeling the negative influence that had set within George about Diego. Making it loud and clear he was going to get him if they did nothing.

George's heavy drinking made it worse. Understanding fully what Diego had done to him. He was ripped off by Diego. Outright and boldly. George was becoming outraged with each puff from his cigar, each snort through his straw, and each sip from his champagne flute. Colombians getting ready to leave, George becoming more and more upset as they were leaving one by one kissing, hugging, and patting him on the back saying, "Goodbye Georgie", telling him it was not a good idea to live in Cape Cod. I had never thought of it like that. They started to say their goodbyes and getting into their limos. We waved as their limos drove off to the airport, it was all over, they were gone. Perhaps they were right.

We were together, and we enjoyed the 4th without them. Our families were very different. George did not want to talk about respect when Diego had just ripped him off for over 1.5 million dollars and, transportation. It was serious, this was nothing to take lightly. "Respect!?" George kept saying, repeatedly. I will show them respect. Betrayal is what it was. We went on to enjoy the champagne, celebrating the 4th of July. We had planned on taking Claire to see the fireworks, so as the evening approached, we got into the car and headed out to see the fireworks. Through the years, we talked about that 4th July and how much we enjoyed ourselves, not knowing what was to follow.

Having to set up deals in Florida. If he wanted kilos they would front them to him but, he would have to go and get them. Flying here and flying there looking for landing strips, living out of a suitcase. Planning the next trip. Feeling overwhelmed constantly hearing about Diego. It didn't matter where George went. Always mentioning to George that he was the man that showed Diego.

Diego had taken over transportation and he was taking it to another level. It was bringing down the price of the kilo. George was dealing with pilots calling off trips to pick up the coke in Columbia for him. There were setbacks. The monies being spent on radios, jet fuel, and traveling all over the country we did with the Cocaine Cowboys, as they are known today.

Leaving for Florida became more and more. Flying back and forth from Cape Cod to Miami was taking its toll. Spending more and more time in hotels was starting to become a huge problem. Do not disturb signs on the door knob, housekeeping not being able to clean because we would have maps spread out on the bed. We were becoming prisoners in a room, planning transportation.

That summer was great. Relaxing and making plans to winterize the house. With George's birthday being a few weeks away, the Colombians were planning a big birthday party for George. A huge bash with a long list of guests. They felt it was their way of making amends.

Family…. you can pick your nose, but you cannot pick your family. George saying to himself out loud, he was not interested in the party they had planned for him. With him refusing to attend the whole time they were planning it, we did not go. It was downhill from that point after he made the decision to not go. My sister and mom so very upset, I could not change Georges mind. He was firm, and he was not attending. Not caring to hear about Diego's success anymore. Filling his ears with Diego, the name was haunting George. He was hearing of the success he was having, the trips that were being made.

Later, that night, William calls and has me tell George how embarrassing this Americano is to the family, and that he needed to know who was really in charge now.

Not good, it was no excuse, even if Diego had betrayed him. George wanted Diego gone.

George mentioning how he really disliking all of them. George decided he did not want to deal with the Colombians anymore, he was trying to get away from them. He would not answer their calls nor his beeper. Little by little stripping him from his dreams and his life making it harder and harder. We started to travel more and more to Weymouth, he had business there. A quick stop at his parent's house to see how they were doing. He loved his parents. He would be gone for days taking care of whatever business, he had pending. George bought an old thunderbird and had the engine re-built. We go back and forth staying up on top of the deals in Boston where he got his name Boston George. We would eventually head back to Eastham.

The last summer holidays. Labor Day weekend. The Cape became empty and quiet. Everyone packed up and left. Charming as it was. Peaceful tranquility from the traffic on the road. For all the vacationers had left for the summer. Fall just around the corner, there was a crisp feeling in the air, along with the smell of the bay.

We called in an interior designer, she came to the house and laid out samples, different patterns, and colors of fabric. We both sat there going through the samples, choosing and agreeing together on what we wanted. Custom made drapes in an orange color tweed fabric that reflected a glow in the living room. Breathe taking. Each room had a unique look to it. Winterizing the house in early fall. Life and love had taken a new meaning now.

Getting ready for back to school, taking Claire and registering her. She was now starting school on Cape Cod. When I walked in, I felt so out of place, I was over dressed being that I was from New York. Running back explaining this to George, he looked at me and said we need to go to the mall and buy some Cape Cod clothes. Talbots and then Filene's department stores, remembering my first pair fishing boots. A plaid blouse and a few pairs of blue jeans. No more dress pants when going out and about town. A total transformation from the New York city look to Cape Coder. It was echoing in the back of my mind about what the family had said. It would be too isolated. Putting these thoughts behind me, asking myself, could I adjust to this? If we were together as a family, I could. It was all good.

The sunset views out on the deck were beautiful. As darkness fell, from a distance you could see the witches dancing around the campfire. As we stood there on the deck he would think how silly it all was. I had a different outlook on it. It was not silly. It was the beginning of the magic. Doing spells on us. Hexing us. A witch coven. This happened numerous times while we were there.

Once again everyone started coming over, his army of men wanting coke, money, or both. He had brought a few guys to the house and found himself having to help them. It was becoming overwhelming.

Suddenly, he wants to get a place away from the house to be alone. The game starts. He picks a Cape Cod house on the water in Wellfleet, it was near Provincetown, a few miles away from the house.

We were caught up in the S & M game. It was the escape. Coke became the helper, it was part of our life. Addicted to the numb feeling of pure cocaine ecstasy. Also becoming addicted to the game. Buying whips and chains. Jumping in the car, heading out towards Provincetown, the wind against my face and a trail of our dust behind to be fitted in a new outfit for Mistress Mirth.

Racing back to the house in Wellfleet, doing more and more coke. Coke had taken over. We continued to play for days being tied up in the attic. The part in the movie with the light flashing on and off. It would have been X rated if they would have put the real story in there that took place. It would make Lady Gaga look like a virgin. Hotel California in the works. You could check in, but you could not check out. Taking coke to another level.

Drug so powerful, it was right off the plane with the ability to change one's perceptive view on life.

It was like having a double personality. Vampires by night. Humans by sunrise. Keep on keeping on, bring the coca.

No one able to contact George. Except for the nanny if she needed to contact me. It was our fantasy hide away. Having total control over George. Allowing myself to play the game becoming a reality. The thin line between what is real and what is fantasy. Coke making it reality. There was no contact with George or from George, any news came through me and left through me. Staying away from the house in Eastham was becoming more and more. No one knowing our whereabouts. It made it more exciting.

It was becoming insane, the upkeep and maintenance of the houses, then one night the nanny calls my beeper. She tells me that a car drove up to the house in Eastham. It was my mother and a companion, more like a bodyguard, sent by William to pick up Claire and with a message to advise George that there would be no more business.

I returned as fast as I could to Wellfleet. To free George from his bondage. Neither one of us could believe what was happening. When we both got back, they were gone. Coked out with no sleep. It was neither a dream nor hallucination.

Message left with the nanny was that if he wanted to keep making money he would have to relocate to Florida. Those were the terms, written in cement. It was upsetting. Claire was taken and on her way to Florida. We packed up quickly and, called for the plane to be ready. We took the limo to Hyannis Port, and within hours, we were in Florida.

There was a car waiting for us. We had a little luggage, enough to change, and a few toiletries.

We arrive at my mother's house early morning. Having an extra key, we let ourselves in. My mother was awake, and she was glad to see us. She kissed and hugged us, it was a huge a sigh of relief for her.

In the morning, George was calling Barry Kane, the first pilot to fly the first load. Barry was living in Massachusetts, being a single parent ever since his wife died. He was a tall and slender man with silver-gray hair. I gave him the nickname the Silver Fox. He had an elegance about him, even as to the tone of voice, he was soft and low, spoke very distinctively. Being a lawyer and a pilot at the same time gave him credit from the cartel. He demanded business be conducted on-time, he waited for no man, and conducted his transportation business very professionally. He too had a place in Cape Cod and Fort Lauderdale. Suggesting to George to meet in Fort Lauderdale where we would meet and talk over breakfast. We left before anyone in the house was up. Leaving in a rent-a-car to meet Barry for breakfast and business.

During breakfast neither George or I really ate. Barry could tell that we had been up for a while, we looked horrible. Our faces were shiny, hair greasy. He looked at us and said neither one of you look good at all. You both look like shit. Your both coked out.

Knowing Barry was right we ended the meeting and went back to my mom's house. We stayed with her for a few weeks and then we decided it was good for us that we all move in together. Getting a bigger place, she was for it. As I look back now. It was her concern about us doing the drug and how Claire is being left with strangers even if they were maids or nannies. It was no life for a child with parents living here and there, no structure. It made her feel better to be watching after Claire, and she was right. Our life was very unsettled at this point. Once again, the packing started as we planned to live together. We found a place. It was a beautiful house on the water with plenty of rooms and space. Finding out I was pregnant, George wanted a family too, both of us very excited. I was eight weeks along. He threatened me at the time and said that if I got rid of the baby he would kill me. I had no intentions of doing anything, but he was serious.

George now needs to go back to the Cape. Alone? I start to wonder and demand that I go with him. He had no choice but to take me. We get back to Cape Cod, missing our home, it felt good to be back. Even if it was only for a few days. It was chilly, and fall had already started. Leaves starting to change colors from green to red and yellow, there was a carpet of leaves on the ground.

We also had the other place in Wellfleet and needed to go there to close the house up. We drove back to Wellfleet with a suitcase full of different devices from the Dungeon. We took the memories and locked the door behind us. We smiled and looked at each other as we got into the car and drove away.

Back at Eastham. William was calling, phone ringing, beeper going off continuously, wanting us back, and did not want us to be long on the Cape. After a few days, we closed everything up with hopes to return soon. On our way, we had to stop by his parents' house in Weymouth. We spent a couple days there and had a great time. Fred his father knew we were going to Florida. After we got into the car, Fred and Ermine had tears in their eyes. We waved good-bye and drove away.

Ermine never turned in her son as seen in the movie, it was his uncle.

On the way to catch our flight we spoke about the new place and how it would be better. Summers on the Cape and winters in the Sunshine State.

Soon thereafter we would all be settled in Pompano, Florida and we could now move forward, making the family happy, knowing we were finally within sight. Pompano was nice, and the winters were a lot warmer. Adjusting to living in Florida.

It had advantages for me. More peace of mind, knowing we were safe, but safe from what? No, we weren't. Now the risks were greater and the upkeep of all the homes was greater too. Keeping up with the lavish life style along with the price tag for it.

George and Derek still doing business on the west coast. Known in the movie as Derek Foreal. He was far from being a gay man. He was a short man with a beard, kinky curly hair, and looking more like a homeless person. He was far from it and very wealth now. I always wondered how he could have felt watching himself portrayed as a gay man in the movie. He was Italian and connected to the underworld through his family.

The family was keeping a close watch on George, they knew the hate he had for Diego was becoming more intense now. Hearing how Diego was setting up deals with different families. He would not sleep and just snorted and snorted, there would be no end to when he would crash.

Everyone was talking saying, "Here comes Georgie. The vacuum cleaner doing lines as long as I-95 north to south and south to north. The crash was sure to come.

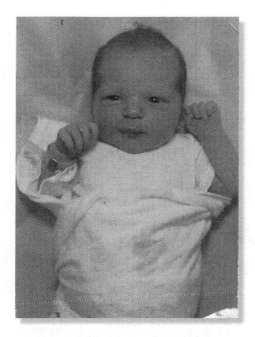

1978 Kristina at birth

Mirtha after giving birth to Kristina

Clara's 1st Birthday

Family after church

George on the run from the Colombians

Kristina and her cousin

Kristina at 3 years old

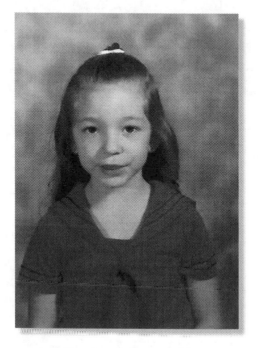

Kristina at 4 years old

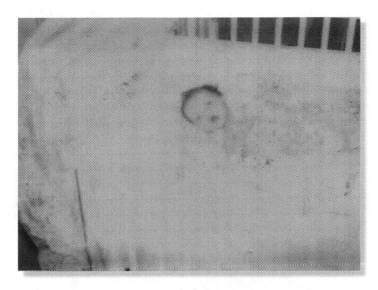

Kristina new born

My sister Martha and husband William

My sister Martha and Mama

# IV

# CRASH

## Dreams blown apart

"Last call!" the bartender would yell out "It's 1:45am, last call." It was time to go to the next place, "Where are we going?" "Where is Cheryl?" "Where is she?" Sweat pouring down our faces from dancing. We had to get that last drink, that last dance. We all would run into the women's restroom. Pulling out the brushes and lipstick, refreshing ourselves, "Here… got the vial?" Pouring the blow onto the mirror "Don't blow on it! Be careful I don't want to have to go home to restock, here let me do it." Taking the straw right up to the nostril. "Put the damn blow up your nose girl." "*Hmmmmmmmmmmm*" that sudden boost of energy, the alcohol doesn't feel like it's in your system anymore. 100% pure cocaine. The look of snow that glitters, you could smell the sweetness, the feeling of numbness all over your body, that drip down the back of your throat, that all too familiar feeling that took over your whole body, and suddenly it was *weeeeeeeee*. It was not cool to use another person's straw. Germs! Yuck! I made sure I carried my own straw, I had a colored straw that matched every one of my outfits. Sheik, wouldn't you say? I also had a silver bullet, so small you wouldn't even notice it. You turn it upside down, blow would release into the cap, and poof... up your nose it went. Only the knows knew for sure. It was from my private stash right off the plane.

Gloria was into everything that could get you high. Pablo's girlfriend, being French, was beautiful and sweet. Being in our early twenties and having everything we wanted at our fingertips. Money, blow, pills, and weed. The best weed was coming in from California. We were all the same age Pablo, Diego, and I. Except for George, William called him the old man. Everyone else was under 30. I feel that was the success of the Cartel. Young was strong and old was knowledge.

Diego would pick up Yamel in his Porsche. Our driver would be there to pick us up too, we flew down to the Keys where we continued to party for days. No one wanted to come down. It was such a horrible feeling, the thought of the crash. You knew when the crash took place, your body could not keep up with your mind, and the mind was racing so fast that you had to stand still, just for a moment to collect your thoughts. Then when the sun came up, out came the sunglasses. Sun beating on our heads and face frying us into crispy critters.

The sticky, sweaty feeling with your nose stuffed up from all the blow. Conversations taking twisted turns, a dark tone; you could feel the weirdness in Diego's voice and see his behavior. It would get scary, that would be the start of the crash after a

4-day run. It was always important to douche the nose, one of the tricks of the trade you learn quickly, until your nose started to bleed, then you had to stop. It was the strangest thing to think about. We lived in the Sunshine State, yet no one had a tan. We never had a tan. The days were spent in air-conditioned rooms with curtains drawn, only using a small table lamp for light. At night, in the cooler air, we came to life.

Like a vampire, but cocaine, not blood, was our supper. Again, we were to be up all night, as day broke again we were safe back in your dark abodes. This frenzy of feeding repeating itself over and over, again and again.

The crash would be inevitable. For George it took days to recuperate, but for the rest of us, being much younger, we could do it all over again, after catching just a few hours of sleep. We would book into a hotel, go out buy clothes, drink, and snort. It was the time of our lives. Little by little stripping us of life and the dream that we once had shared.

Flying here, flying there, we were like feathers in the wind. Whatever direction the wind blew so did we. I remember, one time I was on the plane with George and asked the stewardess to tell the pilot I wanted off the plane, we had one of our grand fights and I wanted away from him. The plane stopped on the runway and I was allowed off the plane. Try that today, you would be arrested and taken into custody. Things have really changed, but the crash is still the same. The crash becomes harder to bear, the addiction stronger and stronger you look for ways to justify it. For the longest it was our cure for all things. Had a cold, take a hit, no energy, take a hit, take your vitamin C now this will perk you right up.

Cure for all things. Drinking and snorting became like breathing air. George had finally become his own best customer and still with a small army. Diego had become king of transportation. George's crash was day in and day out, all he would talk about was Diego. Snorting more and more by the minute.

He never admitted the night at the Castaways about how he saved their lives. George finally puts a transportation trip together, this time the pilot is Derek. It was the best transportation trip we had planned.

Buying a plane that could make the run all the way to Colombia and back without having to refuel, bypassing Cuba and the Bahamas, straight into the country, Boston to be exact. Setting it all up.

Meanwhile, we were also making plans for all to meet in Eastham, Massachusetts. George keeping in touch with his boys.

The time is getting closer and George starts to run into problems. The plane was being stored on the east coast and weather was an issue not allowing for the plane to take off. Not being able to fly to Miami, and not letting anyone know in Eastham that there is a problem. Including the undercover agent that had befriended us that Labor Day weekend.

Willie gets frantic and calls George to tell him the deal is off. They're waiting in Colombia and need to send another plane with another pilot. There was no way George could pull off the trip.

George becomes totally upset. He demands that he be given 20 kilos from the trip for his troubles. Willie agrees. Within days, George had the 20 kilos.

Returning to Eastham, George keeping to himself that he had not pulled off the trip to Colombia. Not changing any plans, acting like all was going according to plan. Letting everyone know that we were heading back to Eastham, Massachusetts. Finally, we get to Boston, there's a limo waiting, my guests and

I would go by ground to meet George and Derek in Eastham. They would fly to Hyannis Port. A change of plans, but we all finally get to the house in Eastham.

The undercover agent pulls out a gun and is yelling, "You are all under arrest! Hand shaking, holding a gun. Within seconds, Marshall came crashing in from every possible entrance. We are all arrested that night and taken to jail. Posting my bail-bond the following day, I was the first to be released. Later that day the others got out, you never saw the real story in the movie.

Kristina, being only two years old, was with me too. She did have to go along to jail with me, but the part when they're taking his heart, in the arms of officer, it did not happen that way. It was not cocktail waiters, it was one man, and only one-man. In the movie where he is sitting there asking for a deal for his wife, there was no such deal.

We were all arrested. Federal Marshall were sure they had gotten the load. There was no load, for the trip had been cancelled. Little did they know. Arrested by the man that had worked on the sting operation to bust us. A state trooper that would party as hard as we did, doing coke and drinking. With him being law enforcement, what kind of reports could he have written? Now still in Eastham lying in bed, having to go back to court. George talking about and making plans to skip the hearing. We both leave everything behind, not even a suitcase, as not to draw attention, for we are being watched. Not fully understanding that at that point, I would become a wanted fugitive. Loving him as much as I did, is the simple reason as to why I left with him.

Just as the crash will come, there are different types of crash. Today I think, and I feel that emotional crashes are the worst and hardest to get over. Not drug induced ones that can either make you or break you. The mind shuts down and it is hard to focus without being scattered all over the place.

The loss of a child, parent, or a loved one dear to our hearts, are those we treasure. Some die in a flash, with those that are still living never looking back. *Poof* out of our lives. Still in one's heart, wondering how this could happen. As I would light my candle, I would focus on the beautiful glow of the candle burning. My affirmation would be as follows; Asking for strength and mercy upon my spirit for salvation. With my spiritual knowledge I knew within, that even the way a candle burned, would reflect on the negative forces being directed my way. Being sent back to where they came from.

Feeling the crash landing on your face, breaking your nose and just waiting to get out of the emergency room to get more coke. Thinking back how crazy it was, playing Russian roulette with a gun and so stoned that it was funny to pull the trigger and hope it was not you. What a degree of madness it was playing this game. Drug traffickers. My horrible crash came behind bars.

Crash of hoping that someone changes, but they continue in the same pattern. A liar can crash one's life for every lie is yet another blow. Lie if you are hooked on drugs, sex, or food. What happens with those crashes? Not all crashes are from drugs. The ups and downs blow after blow.

Setting forth forgiveness is also a cure. Music is also good for the spirit. The newer the songs the better and easier the emotional crash becomes, for the energy too soothes our souls.

One must know that we are in control. The voice we hear alerts us when we know and feel it's wrong or bad. As a child, these are the values thought through generations. Now we have bullies in such a negative force, they were always there, the negative forces making school hard, the gang-bangers, and drug dealers. Even selling pics on YouTube and cell phones. What happened?

Prayers are answered, all in due time. If you were to die right now, do you think of where your spirit will go?

Family Crash of failing in parenting? Work? Careers? Making plans and not seeing them happen? Family starts to crash. A mental and spiritual crash could be devastating.

Getting to recovery is always possible.

# V

# Behind Bars

## Gateway to hell

### Hell, on earth

Little was it known that the feds already knew where
we were? The scene where Penelope is in a bathrobe
screaming "There is no money!" In real life, this is how
it goes down, the part in the movie you never saw.

George wanted to leave Cape Cod and not show up for
court. Explaining they would lock us up at the time, somehow,
I went along with his decision. He contacted a few men he
knew in the drug world. One being Steve. I was jumping bail,
not actually knowing, and being naïve, that once not appearing
in court, fugitive warrants would be issued. Running from law

enforcement meant becoming someone else. Making sure that there is no criminal record with the new identities we are being provided by the Cartel. We were changing the color of our hair and the style of clothes, it was not as easy as we thought or had planned.

It was getting harder and harder after 15 months of hiding out. Doing a deal here and a deal there, no real money to keep us afloat. Trying to stay ahead of the law. Little did we know Steve was already working with the feds. He was setting us up. By the time Steve puts this introduction together, George is already back in jail in Massachusetts on the fugitive warrants. He was coming back from the store after picking up a bottle of scotch. They pulled him over and took him in.

Meanwhile, Steve made a lunch date for us with these two men he knew that wanted to do business. We met Tim and Carl at a restaurant on Calle 8. After being introduced, we sat down. We looked at the menu and ordered lunch. We started to talk about how they knew Steve. Sounded good, so we started to discuss a deal.

I thought I knew what they wanted. He was not interested in blow, but marijuana, and if there was the possibility of getting 100,000 pounds of it. As he was talking, what was racing through my mind was the vans, trucks, and the whole army it was going to take to load, unload, and transport the load. It's thousands of miles away, and nothing like coca to transport.

I knew this because of the transportation George had done with marijuana in the beginning. He also wanted a front, he would put half the money up front and pay the balance when it reached its destination.

Knowing his terms, I knew I could do it. I knew I could get the merchandise fronted to me. All it would take was meeting with a few people and arranging it with them. I wanted to do this deal to help George with legal fees, I wanted to make sure of where the money would be delivered and how it would be handled.

We would meet again and discuss the deal in more detail. We both looked at each other, but there was something about those piercing blue eyes, just as of those of the man who had busted us.

Flashing back to Cape Cod.

Oh, yeah at this point I was flying so high I am surprised I didn't touch the sky. After all my nickname was bird. I flew like a bird and ate like one too. Johnny was the best choice for drawing the females. All women love Johnny Depp, he has that look. Would you have felt the same if it would have been Sean Penn or Matt Damon?

Getting back to the story now.

We parted ways going forward in putting the deal together.

Meeting with my family members asking for a front, knowing the circumstances, listening and agreeing to the terms, asking me and advising me about their fears, not wanting to refuse me what I was asking for, **100,000** *pounds of marijuana*. Once again asking me, are you sure that he is not an undercover agent to be able to come up with this kind of cash. I reassured them that there would be no problems, so they said okay.

Calling Tim planning to meet once again to discuss all the details. We agreed on a time at the same café. We finally meet. We sat down and had coffee discussing in detail on how the load would be transported and the family's terms. Still, there was something about him that I did not like or trust.

All I could think of was reassuring the family that there would be no problems. As we sat there and discussed the plans, I gave him the sample inside a newspaper and told him to let me know later that evening what he thought about it. As I got up, I said, "Don't forget to read your newspaper."

The meeting was done, then we departed. Driving back this feeling overcoming my self-being that said don't do it. Don't do it.

Later that evening around six o'clock I called Tim being that I hadn't heard from him, he answered the phone. "Hi, it's me," I said to him, "the deal is off we're pulling out of the deal, it's too much of an army that we need to do this with and it's is not really going to work out. Too many people involved." There was a dead silence on his end of the phone. He began persuading me to think it over. "You're going to make a good profit."

The money would have been good. The answer was still no. It is at this point his tone of voice changed and said "Okay." For me, it was a relief to call it off.

I knew that I had to watch myself carefully. I had spoken to my mom and she wanted me to come to the house and rest, spend time with the kids. After giving it a lot of thought, I did. You never saw this scene in the movie.

So around two o'clock in the morning, they come storming into my mom's house. We were all sleeping, next thing you know, a flashlight in my face, crashing from coke I thought I was hallucinating.

I could hear, "Mirtha Jung you are under arrest on fugitive warrant in state of Massachusetts, move your arms slowly out from under the covers," as I was coming to, the light came on. My girls were in the bed with me. I was surrounded by assault rifles pointed at the bed. I could not believe what I was seeing. Scared to death that any wrong move I made they would open fire and kill my girls too. There he was, it was Tim standing over me with those blue piercing eyes, getting me out of bed with hardly any clothes on. My mother was screaming at the top of her lungs and the kids were crying. It was an intense moment.

My poor mother, now crying, asking them, "Please don't take her!" Holding on to me, I had to tell her to let me go, "You don't know what they're capable of doing!" They cuffed me instantly, not allowing me to get dressed, and taking me away in this little terry bathrobe with no shoes. Off I went, soon being taken to a building and put in an interrogation room with Marshall, including Tim.

After I called the deal off they knew they had to make their move. They knew George was a drug lord and there was a serious connection with the Medellin Cartel. After hours of interrogation they finally took me to the woman's facilities in Miami where I was processed.

Waiting for my bail hearing, getting lawyers together to come visit me, and go to my hearing. It all happened on Friday. It was Monday now, I had gone to court and was fighting extradition. I had a million-dollar bail. You would have thought I killed someone. Guards surrounding me. Where was I going to go? Afraid I would escape? George was already in Massachusetts. From the moment we left Cape Cod, they knew who we were, and where we were at. You never saw that in the movie either.

Steve the car salesman, another trader, was trying to save his own neck as an informant. Once again betrayal. Steve was already working with the feds, we were his sting. **Unbelievable!** I could not believe it. It was beyond belief.

Later, I had put it all together in Ted Demme's trailer when filming the movie. There were production pictures of Steve, George, and I on the bulletin board. I had never seen these pictures before, it amazing to me. After so many years, how Hollywood was able to get their hands on these photos? It all came together for me now.

Anyhow, there I was behind bars, fighting my case and fighting extradition. Going back and forth to court. I hadn't slept in a month after being arrested. What a crash. At the same time being thankful that I had not been arrested for the hundred thousand pounds in another state, with additional charges.

Seeing the kids during my visits was uplifting for me. My mom would bring them, so they could see me, albeit from behind a plexiglass window. I never thought at the time what they thought about the whole thing. I only knew they were happy to see me, and I was happy to see them. Kristina still very young, but Claire older, they would smile and say, "Mommy we miss you."

For Claire, it must have been strange, not fully understanding being a young child herself.

There were times after the visit I would go back to my pod as they called it, entering my cell I would just lay in bed and cry, thinking, "Oh I'll get out soon." Yeah, not soon enough. Time keeps ticking and the world keeps on turning. Life stops behind bars. Days and nights are long.

My lawyers fighting extradition, with only three days left they had failed to prove a positive identification. All still a daze to me, wondering if Massachusetts was coming to get me.

Bang, the news comes. The door opens to the pod around 6:30pm, the Correctional Officer says, "Jung, get ready you're leaving." All I could think of was that I had only three days left.

Boom, now the flight of my life. When the U.S. Marshalls came for me, it was time to go to Massachusetts and face the music for the charges I had going on there. I asked Vicki, another inmate, to call my mom and let her know they took me back. I gathered my belongings and the CO came to the door and escorted me to the bottom level where there stood two Marshalls, a woman and a man from Mass. I knew this was it.

I was treated like a human by them. The Marshall's advised me that if I gave them no problems and conducted myself accordingly they would not put shackles and cuffs on me as we went through the airport. Promising I would, it made me feel like less of a criminal in public. As we walked through the airport, there was this feeling of everyone looking at me. We got to the gate and boarded the plane on our way to Massachusetts.

Thinking of George, knowing he was already transferred to Mass. Fugitive warrants, we were caught in the middle of it all. George, the Cartels, and law enforcement. Remembering those blue piercing eyes and knowing my feelings had been right. Tim was undercover.

In flight now, the Marshall asked me if I wanted a drink? Much to my surprise, I accepted. I had a rum and coke, with them allowing me to have another one after I was done. The drinks did relax me.

It was a scary flight for me, not knowing exactly where I was really going. Being so far away from my daughters, my girls. They were constantly on my mind. I was heartbroken. My heart feeling as it had been stabbed. *If you can't do the time, do not do the crime.*

During my flight back to Massachusetts all I could think of was George and how they had gotten him. They didn't really know the truth. The difference was, I knew the truth, and I was in the middle of it all. I was stuck between George, The Family, and the Federal Marshall.

It was a red-eye flight arriving at Boston, Logan Airport. Plane getting ready to land, I thought this was a flight George and I had taken so many times before. Departing the airport, we get into an unmarked car. An envelope with papers and whatever was on me the night they came for me is all I had.

So, there I was in Massachusetts now, all the way from Miami, arriving around 2am in the morning.

Once again, treating me respectfully, the Marshalls offered to let me call my mother to let her know I was alright, I was very thankful for this sympathetic action towards me. Looking back, they were decent people just doing their job.

My mother answered, she was upset and crying. It had to be very upsetting to a mother, after all her daughter was being taking to another state, and another jail. I let her know how much I loved her and appreciated her keeping the girls safe. We hung up. At this time, there were no cell phones yet, only payphones.

There I was, in Massachusetts. We finally arrived early in the morning, the ride seemed forever. I was so scared, but I knew the Marshalls wouldn't do anything to me, I was too valuable to them. Finally, they had the key to the Cartels that they were looking for and wanting so badly. Especially Pablo Escobar and Diego.

I couldn't believe I was going through this, pulling up, getting out of the car in front of this brown stone building, one Marshall in front as I got out, and one that followed behind. *I WAS TERRFIED.*

As the door opened, we were following the Marshall in charge. I was in custody again and this time it felt like walking through the doors of hell. Up these stairs, another door opening, a woman sitting at a desk, asking the Marshall for the papers. Signing them, she was now in charge and I was under their custody. After the exchange of papers, the Marshalls were released of their duty and left. Another part you never saw this in the movie. All you see is screaming Mirtha in the car calling George a faggot. I never used that word. It was one of the director's favorite words and it was added to the script at some point.

It was a shock to me being there, being read the rules of the institution, asking me if I had any drugs or anything on me. Now was time to surrender whatever I had on me to them.

Following my new custodian to where the showers were, I was given shampoo that the institution provided. They wanted to make sure I didn't have lice.

I looked at her over and over. I was wondering to myself and couldn't understand why she had no uniform.

The whole time I was thinking that she was a trustee. Asking her why she had no uniform, but had no keys? "Difference between the inmates and us is, we CO's have keys, and you, inmates don't."

The process started at 3am, it was 5am now. I was given a blanket and told to hang on to it. As she opened this locked door, we got to the booking department, where they took your mug shot and fingerprints. They also take inventory and place personal items like your money and jewelry in a manila envelope when being arrested. The last stop before your new cell.

Another locked door opened, you could see this long corridor. The unit. This is where you are taken to a cell. She unlocked the door to the cell, there I was going into this small room with another inmate, not knowing who they were. There was a small bed as I entered the cell, then door locked behind me. I was devastated.

Lock down for 23 hours a day. We were allowed out of our cell for one hour, that was all we got, it was always around mid-afternoon. It was just enough time to make your collect call to the outside world.

It was hard for some of us that had to make long distance calls, it would take up 5 minutes, you only had 10 mins to talk and then it depended on the number of women housed in the unit for that night, housing over eighty women on a regular basis, mostly prostitutes. It was almost always at full capacity in the housing unit. **Packed it was!**

The bell would go off, everyone knew that it was time to return to your cell and be inside as the doors locked and lights went off, it was time for head count. Standing at attention while the CO called your name out, the response was, "Here!"

Locked up, being counted every two hours, as if we were made from gold. You never knew what CO would be on that night. After spending enough time lying in bed, your ears became tune to the jingle of their keys as they walked down the long corridor. You knew what CO was on duty that night.

In the middle of the night you could hear this one CO go into Pam's cell. It was unbelievable that this CO would put herself at-risk with another inmate who was locked up for murder. You could hear the whispering and the moans, it's amazing what goes on behind bars. Drugs and weapons were common place. Syringes brought into the institution by the CO's themselves. Collecting a paycheck from the taxpayers who think their money is being put to good use housing criminals.

The Department of Corrections and Rehabilitation. It is the most corrupt place on earth. It's more like The Department of Corruption.

George and I were able to communicate with each other from one prison to the another. It was amazing how they would come and get me out of my cell and take me to the booking department late at night. George would be on the phone for me. George had a lot of connections. One time, a Sgt. came into my cell. I was in fear, not knowing what it was about. They would let me know that I was being taken care of and watched to make sure nothing happened to me, no retaliations.

Inmates noticing the Sgt. was in my cell was not good for me. I felt it gave inmates the impression that I could be working with the CO's. Getting information as to what was going on in the unit and relaying it to them. A dangerous situation for an inmate I thought, especially me. No one discussed their case. The response to when asked what you were in for was, usually, "I killed someone," it was not time to get personal, nor trust anyone there.

On the inside calling it "The school of life." It was more like staying alive. Women from all back grounds of life thrown together with different charges for their crimes. Murderers, baby killers, bank robbers, and prostitutes. Mostly prostitutes kept the door revolving.

On Friday nights, boy did they bring them in. They came in packs. It was a good way to clean up the streets before a big convention. It was sad for me to see these young girls in this hell. There was a young girl named Vicky that sticks in my mind to this day, she was barely 17 and pregnant. She was waiting for her pimp to bail her out, but Tyrone never came to get her. She was pregnant, she had no choice but to sit and wait. The longer she waited the smaller her chances got to terminate the pregnancy. Who knows who the baby's daddy was, she was a prostitute. I often wondered whatever happened to her. She was taken to another facility once they found out she was under age.

There was a dark secret behind the Framingham prison. It was coed with men and women housed in different units. The rumors were about the winter prior to my arrival. How they were able to get the men out of the institution that winter because of the illegal activities being conducted by the male inmates on computers.

During that winter, the compound had been raided. The women described what they had experienced during that raid, how they told the story was unbelievable. Their fear that night of not knowing what was going on. The march coming down the hall. To hear them describe that it was different, this was an army coming and it did not sound anything like other nights. It was intense, the chaos of screaming women being pulled out of their cells and being strip searched. Their cells being torn apart in search of drugs or needles that some fucking screw had brought into the prison. Visitors were taking the blame, when in fact, it was a CO according to the story being told by inmates.

I was fortunate not to have experienced that raid. I couldn't even begin to imagine. The raid I had already endured of my own had been bad enough. The most corrupt place. All it takes is being at the wrong place at the wrong time, guilty by association.

As months went by, I was still awaiting trial. George would not take the fall, so for 3 1/2 years we awaited trial. The prison was making changes, we were being allowed more time out of the cell, more time for phone calls. They were good changes, the CO's now wearing uniforms. Still, it quickly got to the point that I just wanted out.

At least with a conviction you knew how much time you got. Being on the compound, there was more freedom. I was still awaiting trial, and the fear was we were looking at 100 years. Nothing to take lightly, it was for conspiracy and the connection with the Cartels.

Lawyers were flying back and forth making their appearance in court. Then came the day that the plea bargain was made. George and I go to court and we are finally released.

All the technicalities and all the money that it costs to buy freedom. The judge says, "Wait a minute. They have no money for a place to stay, where are they going to go?" The attorney stood in front of judge and stated to the judge, "I will take full responsibility, Your Honor. I have a gold American Express card," so it was under those circumstances that the judge released us, both of us on probation. Once again, the judge advising George and me and repeating that if he ever saw us back in his court room again, that he would throw the book at us. Those exact words.

Thus, the paperwork started, and we were released. As I walked down the stairs of the courtroom with George, it felt good to feel the sun on my face and the fresh air of freedom. Freedom wasn't just another word, it was a precious feeling.

Later that evening George and I were together again. We were at the hotel room that had been paid for by the lawyers. There was another court hearing the following morning on other charges that were left pending. We talked about what we were going to do once it was all over. We ordered room service. Champagne and lobster for dinner. Knowing that it still wasn't over, soon we would be a on our merry way, hopefully back to Florida.

Things had changed between him and I, especially on my side. I didn't want to be with him anymore once we got back to Florida. It couldn't happen again, time had changed me, and I knew within myself the choices I needed to make.

I explained it to him, of course it was hard for him to accept the change. I no longer had the same feelings for him after sitting in hell for three and a half years, all while facing the possibility of 100 years.

We got dressed and left for court. They were trying to keep us there in Massachusetts, a deal had already been made. At first it seemed that we weren't going to get out but then later that afternoon we were given the paperwork and set free of the charges in Massachusetts, put on probation and given permission to fly back to Florida where the children were.

Their grandmother getting up in age now. It was great seeing my girls again, another chance to do it right. We got to the airport and broad our flight to Miami and left Massachusetts. Leaving Cape Cod, I never returned.

So here we were on our way back to Florida. When we got there, there was a huge reception for us. Of course, all glad to see us and that we were finally out and back. Everyday spent in hell was to protect my daughter's and family. We had been gone for three Thanksgiving's and four Christmas' after all that had happened. Their hopes were to get George started back again with Derek, the connection in California.

There are many types of bars, not all are visible to the mortal eye. Even if you had special glasses you would not be able to see them. These are the type I felt closing tight around me. I felt just as trapped and unable to move as if they were made of steel and set deep in concrete. I felt that I had to get out or die. Florida was toxic.

Meanwhile. I could see that it was starting all over again. Day in and day out, I wondered how much longer I could continue to live this way, getting up doing coke. After all it was going against all those promises we made when were given another chance. The chance to make it right. George didn't know any other way of life but the one he had lived. He decides he is going to set up another deal in Cape Cod. Keep in mind, we haven't even seen the probation officer in Florida yet. The paperwork was still in transition from Massachusetts.

We were arguing back and forth that it was not a good idea for him to return to Cape Cod. Despite my arguing and trying to stop him nothing worked. He refused to listen. He goes back and gets arrested again in Cape Cod with kilos of cocaine.

Another informant turning him in. This was the breaking and turning point for me. I called my probation officer telling him that he needed to let me go to California. If I'm going to make it, he must give me permission to leave Florida because it's getting out of hand. He explains to me that I needed to have a residence and a job. I asked him again to give me permission to go to California. He said, "Let me see what I can do."

Leaving Florida was the only option. After all, I had kept my mouth shut and paid my dues. Freedom had a totally different meaning to me. I had paid in full! I wanted out.

Knowing George had gone down again and the connection with me and cocaine. I was not going to do anything that would take me back, but there was that chance if I remained in Florida, violating my probation could happen.

Thinking about how I served 3 1/2 years awaiting trial, and then released with probation on my back. I knew that it would be hard, especially because I was falling right back into the old patterns of getting up in the morning and doing coke. Staying up all night partying with George, only he was not going to stop even despite all we had gone through. This was the turning point for me.

It took weeks for the response and the agreement between the probation department and me. I was granted permission to leave with no problems once they knew that George was out of the picture. I was free to take the kids to California and start a new life.

George had new charges now in Cape Cod. My determination was to get away from all of those that were still waiting for me to get addicted and trapped. Only this time it would not be so easy, the fear of going back to Mass.

Time to take control, responsibility. My peace was made with the Cartels. It was all different for me now. I started to make plans to go out to California by myself first.

I got ready and put the funds together to help me with the move, so I could leave. Claire was still in school and it was important to have things ready for both girls especially when Claire got out of school. Kristina was still small, and it was better to leave the girls with my mom for the time being.

California here I come!!!!

1983 Mirtha free after serving 3 1/2 years in prison

Clara and Kristina visit Mirtha in prison

Mirtha and Kristina after release from prison

# VI

# WEST COAST
## CA, Utah, Nevada

I t was another chance, another place, a new everything.
I had found the path.

I knew I had to start over again in a totally different place,
perhaps another state. San Francisco, California was the
destination, now I had to get out there. I would have to call and
report to a whole new probation department. It was time to go
to California and not fall into the edge of darkness. Thankful
to god for another chance. No demons in San Francisco, it was
all about getting there and avoiding the negative forces that
were trying to stop me.

I arrived in San Francisco. My priority was finding a place,
establishing residency, finding a job, and reporting to probation.

I talked to my mother every day being that the kids where still with her in Florida. As the months went by I started to fall in love with the city. The cool weather, the ocean, and all the beauty it had to offer. ***The City by the Bay.***

It was the beginning of a whole new scene in the lesbian community. New categories, new labels, and new, codes of behavior. There were lipstick lesbians, there were politically correct lesbians, there were soft butch, and there were hard butch, there were many categories.

It was and still is a city full of diversity. Getting to know myself at the time, I knew there was something different about me looking back. Here I was, in San Francisco, the gay capital of the world. It felt wonderful. I felt I was finally at home. I gravitated towards the gay community since from a young age. Coconut Grove in Florida. Treasure Island in New York. I had also been drawn to Province Town in Cape Cod, even when married.

I thought of myself as a fag hag. Later to find out, the meaning was a straight woman hanging out with gay men. Not being oneself can also be destructive. I was being who I really was. I finally felt at home. As I started to adjust, working and meeting people, I also started to acknowledge that I was gay. I felt free, finally free.

Eventually, I went out with a co-worker named Paula one evening. We went to Amelia's, a once hot spot for gay women to gather, meet, and dance comfortably.

I meet this woman named Darla who was a Mormon from Utah. We went out together. We shared our inner thoughts, both of us knowing we liked each other. She knew I had kids and the fact that she had none would be different for her.

Nevertheless, she would laugh and say, "It's a package deal." Being a gay mother back then was unheard of. The girls would have two moms instead of one. I also had to think about how the girls would adjust. Mostly Claire, she was older then Kristina.

As time marched on, we got to know each other better. With both of us working, we spent what little extra time we had on making plans and looking for a bigger place to accommodate the girls.

I was finally going to have my girls. I wanted them to feel secure after not being there with them for all that time. Looking in areas of San Francisco that had good schools. I finally found a place I was happy with in the Richmond district. It was ideal, once again a blessing.

The girls would have their own room and the schools where nearby. A good neighborhood and the best part, it was cheap and affordable. I no longer had the disposable income I had been used to in the past.

It was a normal job for me now. Getting ready for the girls, once again, it felt like we were starting over. I was so happy, and life was positive. In the meanwhile, Darla was a good, positive energy.

It was the first time in my life I really felt love. The way she cared for me, her smile, the twinkle in her eyes. We saw each other in our eyes. I truly believe it was genuine love. April fool's day she asked if she could move in. I thought it was an April fool joke, it wasn't. She was really asking to be a part of my life. I was ecstatic. Happy.

We got along great. Knowing in a short time I would be sending for my girls, and they too would finally meet her. We had been friends for some time now, enjoying each other's company. Darla was a construction worker, she too had her days with the coke.

Sharing her experience with the drug, she too had come here to feel, and hear, the sounds of the gay community. In those days, you could walk down Castro St. on a Saturday or Sunday and it would be filled with men, mostly gay men.

Darla found a construction job near San Francisco. In 1973, she was making $9.00 dollars per hour as an apprentice. The apprenticeship lasted one year. Once completed, she became journeyman, making $17.00 dollars an hour now. The good money had started for her as she would explain her story to me.

One day, a superintendent approached her about going into business with him as a partner. Darla took him up on the offer, and now she was a junior partner. She had proved to them that she was a real asset and they wanted her to join them, mainly because in those days' women were considered and minority, roughly translated... BIG GOVERNMENT CONTRACTS.

They (the government) subsidized the payroll and forced General Contractors to hire minority subcontractors. She fit right in when she found out about the business partnership knowing this fact. She was not going to be a junior anything in this partnership. Telling them they could find another girl. She demanded full pay, a company car, and an expense account, she got it all.

She quickly built them into a million dollar a year company. She would share the story of her life. It was hard work for her. Being young helped.

I on the other hand, had still had not told her the whole story about my past and the Medellin Cartel. I was finally clean and sober, working, doing the right thing, staying on the path to recovery, and keeping my probation appointments, sharing with them my progress.

The girls would be coming soon. Feeling good, above all things. I was mentally, physically, and spiritually, back on the path to my full recovery. Preparing myself for their arrival, I would countdown the days. I would say to myself, "Only a few days left!" and they would soon be with me.

Darla was getting nervous hoping they would like her. We felt it would have been harder if we had not already moved in together. I was notified that they were catching their flight. I was truly happy now getting ready to pick them up at the San Francisco Airport, parking the car. Entering the airport, I could barely contain my excitement waiting for them at the gate.

I could see them being escorted by the stewardess, Kristina crying and Claire looking like she was 16 years old. Only being 13 at the time, she was all made up. I was shocked to see the amount of eye makeup she was wearing. She looked like an Egyptian Pharaoh, nevertheless, she looked happy.

Hugging and kissing them, then introducing them to my best friend. We got to the house, their rooms were ready for them. They were happy, and I was too. Life, for us, had started again. I loved having my girls back with me. Doing things together, showing the girls fun, taking them to Santa Cruz, and adjusting to a new life and place that summer. A wonderful time.

It was time to get Clara ready and registered for school. I was staying in touch with George, being Kristina's father, I didn't want any problems with him. I was living a crime-free life now. No coke, no blow, as we called it.

Still, the Cartel would send the boys out to visit me, bringing presents, giving me money, along with blow. I was outraged, I demanded for them to leave me alone. There was no more Derek, and I would never go back to that way of life. The visits finally stopped all together. They gave up, and I was finally left alone.

George was serving time in Massachusetts. Soon thereafter he escapes. Once again, the Marshalls were knocking at the door looking for George. Asking me where he was, I didn't know. Advising me to turn him in if I knew where he was. Over and over they were repeating that if I knew of his whereabouts, I had to turn him in, or else. They kept saying if I got caught knowing, I would face charges too and be returned to Mass.

Now he was an escapee. George calls me. I was shocked to hear his voice, he was breathless. I was telling him how they were looking for him and that he should turn himself in. Refusing to listen to me again, I hung up because I knew they had a tap on the line.

Lucky for me, I had already moved my girls to a better area with better schools. George gets caught and returned to Massachusetts with additional charges. It was the biggest bust in Fort Lauderdale at the time, 320 kilos.

Thanking god, I had not been around him. Once again, he was arrested and betrayed by his pilot. This time he would go away for a long time. After all that happened, we lost our jobs and had to move into a cheaper place. Still talking to his daughter from jail.

Now he starts to write the book in jail. Now, once again, he is back in our life. Collect calls going back and forth, sending him money, sending him packages. I kept in touch with Kristina's grandparent, being sure not to let them know what had happened. All of this going on and it's the beginning of writing of the book Grazing in the Grass till the Snow came. It was supposed to better our lives, which it didn't do.

Mirtha arrives in San Francisco

Kristina and George in San Francisco

Kristina Easter Sunday in California

# VII

# EDGE OF DARKNESS

## Trapped and addicted
## Defeating Negative Forces

E dgy, you're on the edge. You're so uptight. The only way to feel better is to take that drink, pill, snort, hit, or smoke. Thinking to yourself, I've only been clean for 24hrs. Strung out, being on the edge. A world of darkness. Whatever the price, even if it cost you your soul. Where nothing stands in the way. Despite all the remarks being made, finding an excuse for every action, in turn setting off a reaction. Darkness all around you. Not a single beam of light. Nowhere to run and nowhere to hide.

The Cartel became stronger and more powerful with their dealings. At the same time, we were becoming addicted.

Addicted to the money and the drug. The kilos where coming in and being sold at a rate of 100 or more per week. Transportation was the job. Setting up the airstrip, flying in and picking up the merchandise before you could be detected on radar. Crossing Cuba as not to be detected by the authorities there. Planning to make trips on Sundays and any other holidays when the air traffic was busy with so many planes making fight plan and crossing the border at free will.

The coke was in demand by the ones that could afford it. Coke was only for the rich. Only those with money engaged in this drug of choice. The supply was endless. Mountains full of the stuff ready to be processed and snorted up the nose. Trapped mentally and physically without any spiritualty.

It was time to introduce, another way of using blow. The idea was from Escobar. He took a cigarette and sprinkled coke on it and there we sat passing it around. A few tokes and you were numb wasted. What a great idea he thought. That's how it started. It was another way to market the same old product. The addiction took over quick and that was the trap. The money and the drug.

It went from sprinkling it, to cooking it. Bazooka! Free-basing, known today as crack cocaine. The one-time high. One time was enough to get you hooked. Transformed into a rock looking like a small round sugar cube, only smaller. You placed it in the pipe and smoked it. The devils dick, as known to the world of darkness. An addiction so powerful that it stripped you of any values, you would do whatever it took to get the feeling, but that ultimate feeling only comes once. On the edge, looking for that high. The more you do it, the more it takes to get you there. We were young and not aware of the trap. **The Edge of Darkness lingering all around.**

Yamel had turned into a Bazookada. She tried to introduce it to my sister, but my sister refused it. I never fell into Yamel's trap, Diego's now ex-wife, we no longer hung out together. The demons didn't know that they had already introduced the edge of darkness to the wives of the Cartel, they were becoming addicts. This was another problem for the Cartel because it was dangerous in the case of a bust.

One night it became so hairy. They had us on watch with bodyguards. The guards walking around the grounds carrying machine guns for protection. Women under house arrest by these men. It was darkness. Especially when a shipment came through.

The greed for money was becoming intense. George was totally out of control. Living in Florida was another world, even though we would be gone all winter.

The night club and night life.

I would get into my silver bullet as the feds described it. Up the road into my secret world. I was hell on wheels, that was for sure. Looking back, it was my denial of who I really was. Living a nightmare and wondering why me? Was I crazy? Yes. I did enjoy my time with the Americano, after all he liked crossing dressing like a girl. In straight circles, they call it S & M.

At times, I would take George and put lipstick on him. Dress him up like a woman. Seems a little sick. Coke was the helper. It became a nightmare with Georgette, yes Georgette was his name when I dressed him up.

She started to collect a wardrobe complete with wigs and makeup. I found myself dressing her and telling her what to wear. Then she wanted to go out and be with me. You've got to be kidding me. It took months before I became insane enough and did take her to Province Town. What a mistake that was.

During my travels to P Town, I had a leather smith that would make any type of outfit in leather I wanted. In the 1970 issue of High Times Magazine, there was this copy of a girl in a black leather outfit never-before seen until then. I had one made, the point was that he had engaged in this game so that he could go back and put a gun to their face and tell them to stay away from me.

Well they did and whenever I would go back to P Town, it was not the same. They lived in fear of knowing me and dealing with me. I had no more gay friends. It ended my trips to P Town. The ADDICTION of coke, the fantasy. Taking it to another level. Being trapped again, in a horrible environment, it was powerful.

My mind, my being, and my spirit. The demon's disciples had tried to lure me back, the addiction of the night life, the club, the evilness from both men and women was becoming intense.

How it came to be and pass.

Evil is so intense. Even for Yamel, who was with a car thief named Diego in Harlem. That was bad, but this was nothing compared to Harlem, it was also full of voodoo doctors and practitioners that practiced Santeria, especially in Miami.

"What drugs is Mirtha on"? It was amazing, and hell not far away. It almost got us, in a way, it did get me. I will go further into that. For me, this is it, where it really started. Even this man I knew committed suicide, he did not want to let go of the evil ties, through addiction and discipline. Falling at the edge of darkness, so much evil. He couldn't let go of his worship to the master of darkness.

The school of life had no knowledge, they were not as evil as these people, who were totally devoted to the demon, for they had laid their nets, the rituals every night.

After a few months I started to think about opening my candle shop and the name. Candles, Oils, & Things was the name I went with. It was quiet, beautiful, and the store was full of all different things to be used in any positive ritual or spells. Starting with the light, it had a good vibe. The grand opening was back in 94, so long ago. By the time the store was being put together, we had moved once again.

However, once again, I found myself having to go to Miami. It was another trap with all the envy and jealousy since they knew there was a book in the works. The original name of the book before Blow was grazing in the grass till the snow came. It was about a horse and lion, him being Leo and me being Sagittarius, the zodiac played an important part in mine and George's life.

As I returned from Miami, I had found great things for the shop, being on a budget, it was great for different uses. Things like egg shell. Magic. That's what I call it. Working with stones, oils, and herbs. Back in the 80's, I already knew the power of the disciples.

George was coming to see his daughter in California.

As the shop started to build up clients with different needs of health and love, seeking what we all want and want to keep, here was this new shop and it was the word in town among the Black and Latino culture, even whites heard about it. Everybody was looking for magic of some kind, so it seemed.

Then as the hours became longer and longer I started to see that negative energy was coming through the door. One afternoon, this woman alone, her name was Maria. She was looking for help for her sons and herself. It was in the stars, she neglected the facts, and her son died. It was so sad. He was playing with a loaded gun and it went off.

As the months went on I started to get tired of the cleaning. The mess when I would get to the shop. There it would be, laying in front of the door. The mess from Mr. Voodoo, with all his followers, and he had many. Then there was the witch doctor, The Burro, as he was commonly referred to. He was way over on the other side of Sacramento.

Chicken blood spatter would be all over the front door of my shop. Pieces of animal liver and hearts. It became routine for me, they would lay it, I would clean it. It was funny, the harder they tried, the easier it was getting for me to defeat them.

One day there were doves that had been sacrificed and at that point it was over. Dove feathers everywhere, head chopped off, it was overwhelming to see this. I made the decision, the store had to came to an end. I felt bad once again, the efforts I had put into it did not come to surface. I wanted to help those in need, my message once again being delayed helping to those in need.

Natalie Holloway in Aruba. I think of her and wonder how she came across a demon herself, not being able to escape the trap. I prayed for her and her family.

Innocence lost. In order to gain knowledge of so much evil in the world, we are unable to return to days of being safe. The days when children could go out without the fear of being abducted, never to be seen or heard of again because of a human predator. Thinking to oneself, it will never happen to me. Never let your guard down, be in control, know your surroundings, don't dwell on it but be aware. We seem to lose having fun with our children and families. Explain the dangers to your children at an early age, better to be safe than to be sorry.

Suffering has become an addiction. Being a victim. It's not good to blame others for the choices we make, just because we are discontent. We therefore become trapped, unable to see, feel, and or make the moment about the present, often forgetting to reward ourselves.

I used to do this to myself. I would cry and wonder why all this was happening to me? Taking control, I would gather basil leaves, throw them in the bath and light a candle to feel the higher forces.

Love-consciousness, is it unconditional love that we have? It is a real feeling, just like that of kissing and holding a baby, or caring for animal as to make it part of the family. Living in the present. We learn to embrace ourselves, reflect on a sunset, or the smell of the ocean. At times, this simplicity brings us joy. We have come to only understand our achievements and possessions. Therefore, becoming trapped, all about money, in an unpredictable world.

Ever ask someone, "Oh, what is your line of work? Okay, you're union, you make good money. Or, "How long have you owned your house? That's a nice car, how can you afford the payments? Girl, how did you get that nice diamond your wearing?", even if you're in debt to your hairline.

We no longer value simplicity. It's all about the achievements and the possessions! If you have long nails, you're a very successful woman. I often wonder how you can wipe your butt with those long nails? Money doesn't buy health. When the time comes it's no longer in our control.

My self-esteem was tested in the movie. Mirtha was made out to be a cold-hearted, bitchy, money hungry gold digger? Being portrayed in that manner for the movie was far from the truth, but it didn't matter to me. I had come a long way, being on the movie set, sharing in the film being made.

I have come a long way since those days. I am excited to share with you how I have survived these demons and hope you will find your pathway too.

End the darkness.

Place a candle in the middle of a white linen cloth. Light the incense, close your eyes. Opening them, light a candle, looking into the flame say out loud, "Jesus remove from me, any negative thoughts and feelings that I have, so I may make an example of thy true love against the edge of darkness. Defeating negative energy. Demons that want my demise, close your eyes. Amen.

It's the feeling of two normal forces. One is positive, and the other is negative. Positive being upwards and negative being downwards. Negative force acts in a direction opposite to what is positive energy. Negativity has its webs and starts to entangle you. Ever seen what happens to a fly when it lands in the spider web? The spider takes the fly and tumbles it around until it turns it into a cocoon and then it sucks the life out of it. In a way it's a good thing for us and for the spider, it eats the insect and there's one less fly for humans, but what about the butterfly? A beautiful, colorful, butterfly caught up in the web. What happens to that beautiful butterfly? It sucks the life out of it too. So no longer is it this nasty ugly fly but a beautiful butterfly gets strangled just as a fly as it tries to escape its fate.

Think of yourself as a butterfly. Negative energy likes no peace, no harmony, no love, and no caring. It creates confusion, chaos, and hate. It smiles in your face and speaks in a soft tone. Thus, the spider and the butterfly games begin.

I'll share with you some of my experiences throughout the years. The strange noises that were heard throughout the house and the unusual behavior of animals. The energy coming through the radios. The loss of heat, electricity, and batteries. Howls in the distance.

Negative forces come in all sizes and forms. Learning their forms and how huge in size their energy is, eventually becoming edge of darkness.

The forces were out in all shapes and forms. Negative or positive energy can come through phones, radios, and TV's, it's electrical energy. Understanding it, knowing how to control it, but best of all, getting totally away from it.

It's there when you go home and shut the door, it's always out there. Think again, is it really? No, it's not. Thinking positive is one of the best defenses against it. A good reason for texting too, no voice, no tone to pick up on. A device that further separates human from sense of hearing. A feeling of being in touch. It's the new way of life for our youth, and they deal with so much negativity.

Terms. You can't judge a book by its cover, same thing with people. Sometimes it's very revealing that we love and care. No turning back, playing it to the end, only to confirm it is evil, and it was evil. A deceiving disaster, known to be a destroyer, without any empathy, there to punish. Just as we choose to allow others to punish us. Pretending to be something you're not?

Accepting a totally different culture, tradition, and religion. Where before, reaching out with love and kindness was a weakness. Being told, "I don't kiss anyone's ass!" I never thought it was kissing ass. I was not a materialistic person. Those around me were, just as it is today.

Do we not start to lie at an early age in life? Telling a lie, or being told one?

As a parent, don't we tell our kids to be good just before Christmas? If they're not, Santa will leave them a lump of coal? Or when they lose a tooth, we say, "Wrap it up in cotton and leave it under your pillow so when the tooth fairy comes at night they'll leave you money under the pillow.

Then there's the Easter Bunny. Ever think why its eggs we hunt? Rabbits don't lay eggs. If not for these lies we tell our children, what would make up their happy childhood memories of those events?

Everyone lies sometime. Let's be clear, there is no time a lie is not a lie. Where "little white lies" are only minor lies. When you're sitting around, and the phone rings. It's someone you don't feel like talking to and your child answers the phone... You wave and whisper "Tell them I'm not here." You just told your child "I's OK to LIE." One of the hardest things to do, is not lie. When a friend or your other half asks you "Does this look good on me?" And it doesn't! What then?

Can we always totally be honest? I don't know the answer, but I do know how badly being lied to hurts. I have been the liar and the one lied too. Once lying becomes a habit, or a way of life, it is a hard habit to break. In my immediate family, I had a family member that you would tell anything to and they repeated it to another family member but would add more to the story making up a totally different version. "Well that was the story according to so and so." Never the original way it was told.

Lies are a trap, once baited and set, you can't get away from it. And, just like the lesson from Escobar having to tell more lies as he was in Colombia and having major problems. It was all catching up with him. The negative he had brought into the world with the flood of cocaine and the things he had done. He was a smart man who didn't want to lose, winning was a major part of his life.

A foul smell surrounds us when we are alone, a smell so foul. Flies in numbers, usually three, was always news of the situation that was going to happen for me. This was a truly negative force. Darkness. Fill a glass of water. Invoke it to the spirit.

A look in a person's eyes that you know deeply, can reveal that there is something not in the light. Sometimes referred to as the evil eye. Those that have it, cannot help it. They could be beautiful people. Loving, caring, and understanding, yet they still have the evil eye.

Loneliness and pain of a breakup is a condition created in our minds. We become regretful and negative to ourselves, we also feel the depression of being alone.

Chemicals in our brain that work like drugs when we are in love. A natural chemical that makes us feel good, just like blow or heroin. Imagine the intensity of a drug and chemical both at work.

Hormonal changes, both in men and women, can also contribute to these feelings and the lack of chemical in the brain from coke or heroin. Drugs are a highly negative force, and so are the medications given to us by doctors. Especially the opiate epidemic. Hydrocodone, Vicodin, oxycodone, oxycontin, Percocet's. Hydromorphone (deluded), Fentanyl (Duragesic).

A partner's absence or hardly being with you. For example, if you leave for work at 5am and you return at 9pm, you're away how long? How much time do you spend with your family or partner if you have one? We make a choice. Is it really about the money or is it that we have a better time at work then we would at home?

Negative Forces start to act in front of you, behind you, above you, to the side of you, and all around your field. Some people call it the aura, the glow, or the shine, once again all these different chemical and hormones. How many of us check our hormone levels? How many of us drink at least 24oz of water every day?

All of this contributes to the negative energy tearing down your body, mind, and soul. Sucking the joy and life out of you. Have you ever had this feeling not being able to breathe because a force had taken over your body? There's a chill when you feel it, a certain breeze at the time. The coldness in the tone of voice, along with the feeling. Bang! It gets you. To the point where you're in bed now wondering if you should just lay there, but the longer you lay there, the worse it is to get up.

Our parents and other adults coax. Example, have you ever received a gift you didn't like? What would you say? "Oh, it's beautiful." Knowing, you will never wear it.

At times we do tell people, but we don't tell children what we mean, in the hope of not hurting them. It's not about lying as we get older and become responsible adults. It now becomes deceiving, and it takes a whole new meaning. As adults, we should be able to understand when we want the truth, but are we ready to hear it? If so, it should be easy to say no. "As a matter of fact, why don't you try on another dress, that one is not becoming of you. So why do we even ask how it looks, when we already know how it really looks? We know what looks good or not good as men and women.

Sometimes we think something looks good, like a haircut, and no one even says a word about it. Sometimes it's better not to ask or to say. It lets us know right away without needing reply. It's like when a man gets out of the rest room and forgets to zip his fly. Do you tell him? Do you make a sign? Or do you just let him walk around with his zipper open? How would he react? Has your makeup eye ever smeared and left you with all this black mascara around your eyes? How many people would let you know? There are times we don't tell a person. Why? Are we embarrassed to tell them? Do we lie and pretend not to see it? Or is it called ignoring?

As she was growing up, I was lying to Kristina about her father having been in a boat accident. I told her he couldn't walk and that he was paralyzed, to spare her the truth about him at such a young age. When he finally got out of jail again this time, she was in her teens.

He showed up drunk the first time to see his heart. It was a horrible experience for her. When she saw him all she could do was cry, in an outburst she was upset that she had been lied to for all those years as she was growing up. Yes, I had lied to her to spare her tender feelings at that early age in life. Was it a mistake? I feel it was, it was a lie!

In the end, the lie that was told to our daughter now became a confession of the truth. I had to confess to her. I was grateful not to tell her he had died after he had gotten arrested. He thought he would never get out and wanted me to tell Kristina he was dead, on the advice of family therapist. I didn't. Thank God.

So, when does a lie become deceiving?

Today there's a different outlook for recovery. It's all in what we do and think. Once again turning the darkness into light. To redeem oneself. What is not good is not of God, it's of darkness.

Once again, alerted by the spirit.

An old saying is, when your neighbor's house is burning watch your own (Cuban). Words that would generate the conversation, envy was discussing how his or her business was not doing well.

The game had started and the abuse sets into motion.

Spirit. Reflections of the spirit through the eyes-only, the negative force totally lost in its own evil doings. An evil doer.

The envy and jealousy. People don't think it's true or believe that it's a real force, a thing.

It's what causes blow after blow. The energy so intense that it is scary and at times, frightening.

There were times, even when I was small, that I could hear spirits. I have always believed that the higher power, or God, is stronger than any negative force, for the spirit protects you. What kind of power is stronger than that?

I also believe the devil does exist and that if there was no such thing then why is there so much evil in the world? Then why have we, at times, had the feeling of, or the smell of, we are not alone. It is a strange feeling that over comes our being. It's a déjà vu, thinking have I been here before? I have. Have you?

Setting white flowers in the center of the room. Person comes over and the flowers die. A removable negative force in vision.

Being in sync with each other, being connected, being one. When we don't listen, it puts us in defense mode, which is negative. Respect is one of the fundamental necessities of positivity. It reduces the occurrence of stonewalling (refusal to talk or listen), a negative force. Negative forces can tear down the respect between two people. The force itself, as like in humans never being there for one another. Using energy and magic, always saying what they think or feel behind the person back. Spinning and stirring it up, saying one thing and doing another.

Through the years I have managed to continue cleansing and have made my own formulas using oils and herbs. Burning lavender along with frankincense, formulating different herbs and techniques to set a peaceful and restful environment. Setting coconuts and a bowl of fruits to refresh the home of negative spirits. The milk of the coconut sprinkled outside the door to remove negative energy. The lighting of a white candle, placing it up high on top of something if possible. Making sure to keep it in a safe area, out of the reach of children.

Negative forces will always be there and on the attack. Especially when creative visualization comes to play in our minds. Like the daydreaming stage, a place to go in your mind, somewhere happy.

Heavenly father brings peace and love to those that stand against us while waiting for the fall. Humbly asking to forgive me and those who have offended thy mercy and love, bestow my spirit, saying these things in the name of your beloved son Jesus Christ, amen.

# VIII

# NAPA

## Beginning of the end

We had to move from Sacramento for many reasons. The main reason was to get Kristina away from the influence of the gang bangers and felons that were going to the High School she was attending. Her not wanting to join the gang, the retaliation was throwing a six pack through our living room glass window and breaking into our home while trapping her in room. It took 13 mins for the police to respond because of our fear of a drive by. Leaving is all we could think about, there was no protection from a bullet.

The book was re-written by Bruce Porter as the days unfolded, still with us trying to maintain a stable life. It was all out of control.

The movie now being talked about more was finally becoming a reality. No one knew of our past life. Thank god. Her father's reputation, not being positive, could have created more chaos for Kristina. Having to go to the school to address the situation with the principal, he said he would have to report me, and she would be truant. I stood up knowing the conversation was over, thanked him and walked out. The fear of knowing that even the gang task force was afraid of the gang bangers, only giving us a button to push, if they were to come back.

Praying to my heavenly father to help us because in the back of my mind I had to go back to the store.

I remembered at that time I was being bombarded by the evil doers, a stressful situation to say the least. The negative forces had reached us, and this time it was Kristina who was in danger.

Looking everywhere, filling out applications, submitting them as far as Benicia, CA. We were desperate. Needing to find place, looking everywhere, finally there's an ad in the paper. We make the necessary calls to get together with the owner, setting up a time and place to meet in Napa.

Going to see this place in Napa, it did help to have the money for the deposit and rent. There we were, signing on the dotted line, we moved in as soon as possible. The place was great, it was beautiful, and it even had a pool. It was a fortress behind these white brick walls. There was a front door to the side of the brick wall. Opening it, there was this beautiful walkway entrance to the front door of the house. Bamboo trees along the path, as you got to the front door. The security was exactly what we needed.

After registering Kristina in high school, she was able to catch up with school her junior year so that she could be on schedule to graduate. She loved her new school, she was happy that everybody was so friendly, and she could not believe how friendly they were. Her grades started to improve dramatically.

Living in Napa was nice, but it wasn't all that it's made up to be. You never stop to think about the wineries and all the chemicals used to keep the grapes free of bugs essentially contaminating the atmosphere. Humans living there are always breathing this in the air.

You see the hot air balloons flying and the rows of grapes along the way as you head towards Calistoga where the mud baths are. It is a beautiful part of the country. It was quiet. The property value started to go up and we liked it there, so we met with a realtor who wanted us to buy a house in Napa. It was a good price and a small down payment for an old house that was considered a fixer-upper.

We used whatever money was available to qualify for the loan. The lawyers finally call with the news the movie is going to be made. I needed to sign papers and contracts.

During the time Darla and I were together, even if she had a good job she didn't have good credit. For years when we first met, I had to write letters to her creditors, make arrangements, paid little sums that had been left pending trying to fix her credit, and hoping her credit score would come up.

Having bad credit made it hard. We had a hard time getting through major problems that had been brought on by both of our exes. For one reason or another there was always someone there to trip us up. With a little money from the movie deal, Kristina finishing high school and working, we called the realtor and made an offer.

Darla was going back to work after being on disability due to a job injury. No one around us thought we could do it. Saying, "You guys can't do it." We did it. We get the house. The house needed a lot of work. The kitchen had old metal cabinets and the stove was covered in grease. The walls were filthy, it took us a month to clean the place up. No remodeling for us at the time because there was no credit.

I was surprised and excited at the same time. Letting everyone know that the book was going to be made into a movie. Wanting to share the good news. It was not good news for those around me. When I look back again, I could feel the intense energy of envy and jealously.

Strange things started to happen. Knocks on the wall, waking up and being so scared, thinking someone was breaking into the house. Lying there wondering why the alarm wasn't going off. Dishes falling, for no apparent reason. The radio turning on and off by itself. It was scary, but I know there is no greater power than that of God, it helped me. The smell of rotten eggs knowing there was no sewage problem.

All of this going on while the movie is being filmed. I was trying to keep control over this situation, spooky things going on making you wonder why all of this is happening. Only now so intense it was making it hard to even enjoy the project.

Sharing these feelings with Teddy, thinking to myself, he must think I'm on drugs. He asked me once "Are u doing drugs Mirtha?" It was shocking to me, I said "No Ted." Lighting candles and burning herbs to remove whatever negative forces were being directed my way. I lost focus of the negative force. Phone ringing and no one on the other end. I was fighting what could not be seen. Mentally and spiritually these where the signs of what was to come. Ted's Demme death. The beginning of the end, Napa. We made the decision to sell the house after his death. It sold within weeks at a good price, giving us a profit to invest into another place. It was another chance to get over his death and what turmoil had happened. We moved up further north past Calistoga to invest the money from the sale of the house. Leaving a piece here and a piece there.

I had brought my mother here from Florida. She was becoming more and more ill and I couldn't keep flying to Miami, knowing it would be a trap if I continued to do so. I went and got my mother and moved her to Walnut Creek, CA.

I spent time going back and forth from Walnut Creek to Nice. I had to check up on the house to see if my belongings were still there. It was not the same going up there anymore. At night, it was very dark, and it was large land. The ride up there was a nice either way you went, up Highway 12 or around to Highway 16. Route 12 was longer, and it had more winding roads. Route16 was along a creek and when you got to Hwy 1 and made the turn, you knew you were out in the country. It would have worked if we had planned to live there and make it work.

As the months went by and fall approached, it got harder and harder to go there. The leaves on the trees changing colors and falling. The drives became longer and more spread apart. I was able to pay the electric and gas bill for a few months. I had no money and had to pawn my jewels so that I could pay for the bills that I could and gas to get out there. I took the bus up there a few times. Staying alone was horrible, I knew I could not live there with the memories that had been left behind. Kristina and I got caught up in all the driving back and forth from Nice to Walnut Creek, we were trying to find a direction.

I would go to the city and stay there for days. No one would talk about it, all they could do was lend me money and keep me company. It had been the only place I found refuge. My gay family, gay life. Now it was coming down to making a move. I had to go back to the house pick up my valuables, things I had from the movie. A lighter Johnny deep had given me while filming blow.

Yes, I was his wife. He would kid around with me and say, "You're my wife, right?" Being around Depp was a wonderful experience. To see and be around this famous person and learning how human and down to earth he really is.

The plan was to move closer to Walnut Creek, until I was able to find a job. By October I had found a job and started looking to find a place to live. Taking care of my Mom, Kristina could not handle the driving anymore. By the time January had come around she was back with her husband and it was hard moving around with a baby.

It was nice to get there before the sun went down. On our last day before we left, Kristina and my granddaughter Athena were out in the back yard, Athena loved it. Keeping the yard up, the walnuts were now falling. I remembered how Dave loved walnuts and how we picked up all the walnuts, they were so meaty. Got a box, filled it up, and I mailed it to him. As the winter came the numerous trips there became less and less.

Then suddenly Darla called it had been awhile. Things were calmer by then, but still painful. We came to an agreement. She was not coming back, and it was time to put the house up for sale.

Perhaps I should have stayed there and bought her out, but I didn't have the funds. I just could not deal with the overwhelming feeling that had been left behind, so negative. I felt the vampires had entered without knowledge and had stripped the house. All these empty spaces where the book cases were. Gone, along with empty wall space where pictures hung before.

Not receiving any money after the movie made things hard and it was overwhelming. Being lied to with false promises was not going to make the family I had so much wanted. No matter what I tried to do, it seemed no one saw the good. Looking back, I allowed myself to believe in all the wrong people.

I have been alone, alone is a state of mind. We are not alone, if we have God in our lives. Often- times asking myself if I should be dead? How and why am I still here? It's to share my life experiences with you.

When I look back, there was nothing I could have done or changed. Only knowing that I had stopped doing my rituals and let my shield down.

Prayer has always been my salvation, it's really in His hands. When life gets out of control you must turn over to the higher power. It is what it is, no it's not! As the days passed, I found myself helpless. I was lost and embarrassed. It was very painful. For the first time, I knew what it felt like to be left by a partner. In the past, I had always done the leaving. Karma was hitting me square in the face. I should have known better. It had reminded me of when I left. When I came out.

The realtor called from Nevada. He had clients coming to the house to show it. It wasn't long before it sold. I think it was less than a month, at that time houses were still going up in value. Finally, the place was sold and once again it was time to move our things out. Darla's older sister went to see the movie. I always wonder why? Wondering how she felt about it. I still don't know why she did. I was the woman who had taken their little sister, their daughter. I was the evil one, living a life of sin. Doomed! Oh, what it must be like to have child damnation.

Homosexual's, queers, lesbians, dike, butch, and all the other stereotypical labels. It was never considered what it should be, two people that fell in love. Love is so powerful when it's real, being torn down because of who we love. Love to me comes in all colors of the rainbow. Could it have been any other way? No. I don't think so. The pressure of it all for her. Especially being married to Mirtha. A movie Blow, a movie portrayed about me. A movie that people knew was about me was not true at all? I was feeling as if I had sold my soul, and all for what?

Kristina on set as a court reporter

Kristina in hair and makeup on set

Kristina and Johny on the set of Blow

Kristina, Johny and Mirtha on the set

Mirtha arriving to premier in her Limo

Mirtha in California

On the set with Johny Depp and Penelope Cruz

On the set with Ted Demme

113

The house in Napa

# IX

# FAMILIES

## Love and Hurt Moments Shared

Y ou can pick your nose but, you can't pick your family. Families, a basis or foundation as to where we originated from, with hurts so intense that we come to realize even our parents, uncles, aunts, grandmothers come and go. Some of us are blessed with family and some of us have none. Love and hurt, memories that remain in our hearts and minds.

Looking for family help, apathy, but there was no one. Hearing their voices over and over echoing through my mind. One way or another it was always no. If we could we would but we can't because we are going on vacation. Let us balance our checking account and we will see if we can help you. Stringing us along. Ever stop to wonder if the help would have come when needed, what the outcome might have been?

I never forgot that helping was putting a band-aid on a problem to save one's assets as a family. If you have a cut, you clean it and cover it to heal it. "It was simply another rejection." One more way they could show their love. As the years went by, we managed. We never asked again. Clean and sober now for over 15 years, it didn't make a difference to our family.

Family was so important to me. We had our own family now. A few years had gone by now. Our families knew we were together. We were happy and raising our children. It was the happiest time of my life.

Going through recovery takes will, but also takes being able to deal with issues, as we call them today, having a partner that shares with you every feeling. Love that is unique, being one like we were, all was going well, our parents started calling writing, being lesbians in those days was scandalous especially with children, just taboo. Both of us coming from strict religious backgrounds, the letters went back and forth, the calls were at least once a week, the happiness we felt. Finally, a feeling of family unity!

During this time, life felt so happy. Unaware of the darkness that would be waiting with their nets to catch us, trap us, and destroy our togetherness.

It was a better life for me and my children. Especially for me. I was finally away from all the hurtful memories of George, although he did still have a lot of love for the family. There are times when looking back I acknowledge the pain the family also caused. How senseless it all was. Family, the Medellin Cartel.

My mother was unhappy here in California. After all the years she had spent in Florida, now in her 80's it was hard for her to relocate. I understand now that the older you get, the harder it gets to move. One time my mother called her sister practically begging her to please give her a room and that she would help with money.

I had just come in and picked up the extension to hear her sister say Clara say "You can't afford to live here. There were tears in her eyes listening to all the reasons why she could not return. My beloved mother was hurt to know her sister didn't want her there. After that, she never called her again, she was crushed.

Her other sister loved her so much and there was nothing she wouldn't do for my mom. My mom was living alone now when they had always been so close. She would make sure to call her every single day and visit with her, I too loved her dearly. She was a good woman. A good aunt, mother, daughter, and wife. Eventually she passed, but my mother never forgot her. All the things they had gone through as siblings, their love never changed. Clara, my mother was blessed by being the older sister.

Her first granddaughter loved her very much too. She would come out from Florida to visit her. There was a special bond between them. I always knew and felt the love they shared. Always calling her. There was always the presence of happiness and love felt with her first granddaughter, when she came to visit, being the only one to come out, because no one else ever did.

At the time of premieres, Kristina being unable to go, as she was due at any time with her first child, we were happy. Sharing in the event was my oldest daughter Clara, my niece, and an old family friend by the name of Bo. I brought along my mother and the real-estate agent that had sold us the house in Napa. Darla was there also.

I dressed in a beautiful white gown to go with the white carpet theme. The idea was Johnny Depp's. He thought it would be cooler than a red carpet. We all looked stunning. Sharing this wonderful event with all those that had come along on the journey. It was awesome. As we got ready to proceed to the premier, I knew it would be and event that no one would forget.

All the cameras flashing as we got out of the limo. Cher exiting her limo behind me. Finally, the dream was coming true. As we took our seats and it started, Teddy comes on stage to give the family a tribute. As the movie rolled, I saw myself sitting around all these famous people watching the movie. It was amazing to see everyone enjoying it. As it ended, we filed out and, on my way, I was able to stop and say hi to Cher. She was with her husband Greg Alman.

Later the premier was followed by a party, we all attended and met more stars. So many people, it was a great moment for us to share together. Party after party, it was a night full of fun. We even went to our rooms and talked all night about the event. The next day we left, and we were once again back to our normal lives, only now with wonderful memories we had shared.

Returning from our event, the premier for the movie Blow, Kristina was now in the hospital soon to give birth. We went to see her and what was funny is she had gone into labor was the last we heard, but when we got there she was jumping on this huge red ball. Inducing labor to give birth naturally, only to find out later that evening that it was not going to happen.

Later that night she had Athena. We all rushed to the hospital to see the new born baby girl, she was cute and healthy. The next day I went out and bought her crib, it's said to be bad luck to buy it before the child comes home.

George calls and is told he is a grandfather. He was happy, you could hear it in his voice. So was Ted, they were both glad to know the baby had been born with mother and child doing well.

We had a lot of good family times through the years. Christmas and Clara's girls, it was always fun during the holidays and my mother was always here for the holidays making them extra special. One New Year's the family shared in happy memories while taking them to the zoo, and the movies.

It still saddens me to know Clara decided not to be a part of Kristina's and my life. She was never able to see or understand any of the effort it takes to stay clean and sober.

As years went by, our families knew we were together, they knew we were happy, and we were raising the kids. It was the happiest time of our lives. The excitement of our parents finally coming to terms with two women raising kids. Going through recovery takes will, but it also takes the ability to deal with issues of being in one's own skin.

Sometimes living in the moment is lost by wondering about the future that we have no control over at times. Spirituality is the most important ingredient to focus in the recipe that feeds the spirit with positive affirmations and prayers. Taking a chance in trying different techniques, the spirit will come, and you will feel the difference.

A loving memory. Sharing a special moment.

Darla's father cutting and peeling carrots, my hands turning orange… laughing for the first time, I was sharing in a wholesome, loving, family surrounding. Being a city gal, I had never canned anything before that day. Love and hurt, memories that remain in our minds and heart, some of us are blessed with families and some of us have none. Accepting one's gender, sexual preference, and not feeling left out.

When I was in Hollywood, the stage production crew would ask me, "How did you do it?" I replied, "God and the presence of spirits that have passed on. Who and what they were for us. That being more than of mortal life, their unconditional love that has now been passed over to us while they are waiting in paradise."

The production crew told me they had never met the real person of the story that was being told.

It is important that you keep your journal too. I have recorded the different techniques I have used and have been successful with over the years.

Beloved family friend Bo Phillips

Grandfather

Grandmother

Mirtha's Aunt and Uncle

# X

# Slipping & Sipping

## Relapse

There are many ways you can slip, you may not realize how close to the edge you are. Slowly you start to think, "I can have one drink it has been so long", and "I'm fine." You can go for years and not drink or do a drug, then the special occasion happens, or a friend tells you, "You're not a druggie or an alcoholic, you say, "Of course I'm not, it's been years and just one won't hurt a thing." Thus, starts the slip and the sip. If you're not aware or just simply, in denial. Disease as time goes on, becomes the illness.

It starts by going out with people that do. Seems that there are those that feel they are better than you, because you have a drinking problem. These same ones are so unique, they say

"It's ok you deserve a break. It's been a long time, you owe it to yourself, one won't hurt," and before you know it, you are convinced that you can handle it, and there you go. As you start sipping you are now slipping. Then no longer slipping but falling. Thus, total relapse.

Support is very important. "Who needs family? All you need is a sip." Relapse comes different for all of us.

In today's time, we deal with addictions to prescription medications. Vicodin, the leading drug of choice, followed by oxycodone, Xanax known as Zanies, ambient, oxycontin, fentanyl, Percocet, deluded slipping into a new legal addiction. A pill in the morning to feel better, another one for pain, and there we have it, you already started a different kind of relapse. Waiting to see what happens, even death, just as in the death of Michael Jackson, Nicole Smith, and Whitney Houston. All stories from here of late, so that puts you up to date as we continue to read through the chapters, getting to recovery.

Directing one's energy through the forces with help from the universe. Forcing our senses and the communication with our inner spirit. The smell of liquor, amazing as it may seem. The sense of smell, the spirit knowing right from wrong, slipping again into the negative thoughts and negative patterns. I have faced so many of those days, and I will continue to face them.

My serenity came from setting up an altar. I would take that energy and invoke my healing. It worked, here it is 35 years later.

Changing the slips, for they're coming in. I was surfing through YouTube for anything written about me, looking for false video representation of who I am. I was shocked to see that a prominent professor could invoke bullying. It was very derogatory to make mention that I was a crack addict. I never did crack, so for him to put it on YouTube as his own little movie, was beyond belief to me. Mentally I would think, why would he be directing bad energy to cause my slip?

It seems George always got a deal from the government. In the movie, they make it seem like he had only been arrested once. However, all because of his way of life, he was trapped in the addiction, thus causing himself to slip to the edge of darkness. He was arrested over five times.

## Blow after Blow
## Stand strong against the odds

Blow has many meanings, in this chapter.

As I walk down the street, I think of so many things. Do you ever stop to smell the roses? Saying a friendly hello, or do you just go on about your business? Helping an elderly person cross the street? Giving your seat up on the bus or train to a pregnant woman? Showing humanity.

As the movie came to life all around the country, you could see everywhere in big black letters BLOW. Up above the entrance to the theater. It's a very different feeling when the movie is about you, guilt by association. Teddy had mirrors designed, they were controversial. People feeling it was done to promote coke. There were only 2,000 made, as I was told. They gave me one, I still have it too.

For me, the blow of Darla leaving, telling me she would return by the 4th July was difficult. Her parents were sick, we were running out of money, and neither one of us had a steady income after the movie. Darla had not seen her parents for years. It was her choice, knowing how they felt about her life style. Funny how all that changed. Assuring us that they would help and to bring the house papers with her.

They gave her a job also while she was there. She was fixing their house, saving money for them, having their walls taped and finished in a smooth texture. Darla kept in touch. Gradually, the calls became less and less. The excuses were endless. She was out, or working, or her cell had no signal. Calling like as if nothing was wrong. Thinking to myself how wonderful it was for them to finally accept us and help us out, for the first time in 19 years.

They didn't. Suddenly, all calls from Darla stopped. She left me with ten dollars to my name. I started to call to find out when she was coming home. Her mom answered the phone. In these exact words, she said, "Darla is home already." I said, "What?!" She repeated it again, "Darla is home, Mirtha." It was a slap in the face hearing these words come from her mom, and not her. She led me to believe that she was coming back, when in fact she had planned to stay there and not return.

It was a cold conversation. I go to the house, all these empty spaces, at first, I thought the house had been broken into, only to find out that she had left. It was a heavy blow. I'm surprised it didn't kill me. There was no regard for how I felt, after all the years we had spent together with no help her from family. This is how it was going down? It was months before she called after that.

Not knowing what the real reason was for her not to return. I was left out in limbo. She had already made plans with her family, without a word, she came to the house and took her belongings. It was over. I wouldn't have ever expected that from her. Knowing how we would handle ourselves in a crisis. At first, I felt my world had crumbled. I would cry and cry going over and over her lack of honesty with the situation.

Breathless, hopeless, and abandoned. There were no acknowledgements or rights after being her wife for 20 years.

I would cleanse, burn my candles, and say my affirmations. It made me stronger, and I didn't have that slip.

We all have dreams. Believe in your dreams, for dreams do come true. Stand strong against the odds, no matter what the blow.

George never paid child support, he was always locked up. He never took his daughter to school and never kept his word to his heart, as you were made to believe in the movie. This was another blow, this time for Kristina, never having her dad there for her. Neither one of my girls ever had a father that cared for them.

In today's world, having no insurance, losing a child or loved one is a heavy blow. Losing your job, not being able to keep your home. A divorce. Living from pay check to pay check. In a world where only the rich become stronger and more powerful.

All these blows facing us every day in life. In a world where there is no humanity, no love, no caring for those that struggle, and not knowing how to handle a crisis. These signs are telling us something. When you're feeling choked, remember that God does not strangle us. It's a process to make us stronger in faith. Learning from the pain of hurt, standing against the odds, blow after blow.

These were the blows I endured, but I continued to pray. Years later, life is still full of blows.

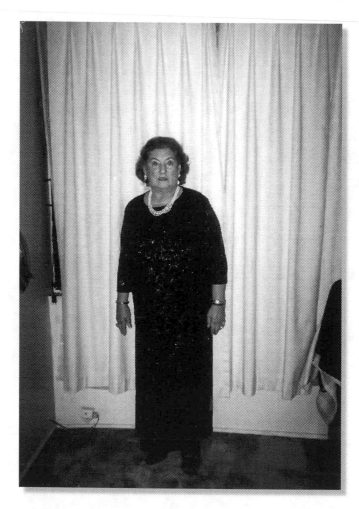

Mama

# XI

# FORGIVENESS

## Setting yourself free

I n the 12 Step Program it says, "You must say you are sorry to all the people that you have wronged to get forgiveness, and that may be true. I feel you must forgive yourself before you can ask anyone for that gift. You must also be prepared not to receive that gift. Sometimes, the hurt is too deep. Applying techniques in my life, is what I used to set me free.

Also, in the 12 steps, the 3rd step is turning ourselves towards a higher force.

Out of our control. Do we not know how to turn ourselves over to the higher power?

In the end, it comes down to the higher power. Accepting ones wrong doing. If you go to jail and you serve your time, are you not to be giving another chance? Does this mean a sex offender should have another chance? Violent criminals? Or taking a life, which is murder.

If we are to achieve eternal happiness in the hopes of seeing our loved ones, are we not first forgiven by the higher power? Everlasting life.

A gift? Yes, a gift one gives to oneself to start the process of closure. Set yourself free. Invest in the most valuable investment in your life while you are here. The spirit. Make sure your investment pays you double the dividends. The key to the gates of heaven or the keys to the gates of hell? You have the choice. Make the best investment in yourself, for yourself.

It took years to forgive some of the actions that people had taken against me. Remembering the time, I was so excited to go to Nevada and perhaps live there. I took a Greyhound bus there and it was a long ride. According to housing market value, it was cheap to own a house there, and with Darla's brother-in-law giving her work, it was a good idea. We were losing hope of buying a house in California because the prices were going up. The good money Darla was making was being eaten up by taxes. It was a great idea to buy a house, so she could save on her taxes.

It was an adventure. It was my first time going to Nevada. Wanting to be around family, we finally planned on making the move. I was so excited, finally we were going to live near family. Blessed are thee that have family that care. As the story unfolds, we saw house after house, there was one that we liked. It was beautiful, peaceful, and affordable. It was huge also. There was a mountain view from the backyard. It was perfect for us, but it was not the one her sister had in mind. The one she liked felt like I was going to be living on the little house out on the prairie. There were no lights and no streets. We spent a few days there. There was this cage with rabbits. Her brother-in-law took us out to show us the rabbits, they were so cute. We go back inside to join her sister. As we are sitting there, a horrible cry. I ask what that is? Darla looked at me and said, "The rabbits are being killed, cleaned, and to be wrapped up to be put in the freezer. Huh? Oh, there's no way I'm going to wrap up the rabbits that I had just seen. Poor Bugs Bunny I thought. It was not good. I had never heard the cry of a rabbit being killed. They could have waited till we left. Later in life, her bother in-law ended up taking his own life.

As for me… in 1996 I was in the passengers' side of a Chevy Luv. We were involved in a car accident; A truck struck my side of the vehicle. It folded my passenger side door. BANG! All I could see was the grill of the other truck. It was like looking at Jaws with its mouth wide open and coming for you. After the bang, the truck came to a stop. I sat there knowing I couldn't move, drifting in and out of consciousness. Drifting through this tunnel of white clouds in total bliss. There was this light, it had a glow that was beautiful. No drug on earth could give you that type of feeling. As I started to drift, I heard this voice saying from far, far away, "Don't leave me." Crying, I could feel my spirit leaving me. Then suddenly, I started to go back to my body. I feel like that was an after-death experience for me. Dr. D. a wonderful woman doctor, said to me at the time that, "Only 1 out of 37 people survive this type of accident.

When I was with the Cartels some of the workers would call me Lady Iceberg. I was so cold and hard core. At times there was no forgiveness. I was ruthless at times, without question. Wondering how it had gotten to this level? Betrayal cost you your life. The fear set forth, was the reason for the respect that you gave. You did not cross them in anyway. There was no forgiveness. Their investment was for self-destruction.

They were all paying dues. I hope they made it in time to ask the higher power forgiveness. I feel so blessed these days in my life. I feel an inner peace. I have made peace with myself.

Forgive then we must try to achieve self-forgiveness. One can never rely on anyone to forgive us. Therefore, it is so important to start with self, and work towards the balance of your spirit, body, and mind.

# XII

# Everlasting Life

## The Finale Death

The finale comes in different stages and settings. Along with a different act. Some people refuse to talk or share about death. Some are scared and then there are those that get ready for the big-event. It's between you and the higher forces when the transition begins. Praying through the years, my prayers were answered.

We started off with a good New Year. Happy and full of new dreams. Hope was strong. We were planning on moving into a new place again.

On Jan. 31, 2011 the doctor's office called, since my mother had blood drawn the previous Friday. They wanted her taken to the hospital as soon as possible. I took her in for the blood work and they had come back with a problem in her liver. She was refusing to go, I had to force her.

We get ready for the non-emergency ambulance to pick us up. As we enter through the emergency room entrance doors, the doctor on duty looked at her, she was turning yellow and the doctor just wanted to send us home with hospice. I was in shock that she didn't want to tell me what was wrong with her. "My mom was 95, and had lived a long life," was her reply. I called Claire, and she suggested that I remain there till they found out exactly what it was.

I took her advice and demanded for them to tell me what was wrong. It took days, by then my mom was becoming weaker. Her doctor said it could just be stones, it would be a simple treatment and she would be good as new. I was having to demand for them to tell me what exactly it was and why she was turning yellow. After all the tests results were back and her doctor reviewed them, she called me in for a consultation.

After meeting with the doctors, her primary doctor confirmed it was cancer of the pancreas. We trusted and respected her diagnosis. By now it was Feb 4, 2011.

It was all over. It was a rush to get her home. It was a Friday. Things move slowly on Fridays in a hospital. I came back to the room and the look in her eyes, spoke for her. She said, "There is nothing they can do for me, huh Mirtha?" She knew inside. I, with fear, denied that there was a problem, and told her it would be best to go home and allow the nurses to come and do what they had to, just as they had done in the past. Still with that look in her eyes, all I could think about was getting her out of there.

I didn't want to waste what little time we did have left to be together. Her doctor was a wonderful human being. She got things moving fast, cared for my mother, and grew to really love her. I knew deep down, the spirit talking to me, that she knew she was going to die. In no time, we were home. I was calling for the priest as quickly as I could, making the arrangements for her last rights.

He came over as soon as he could. She was blessed during this time with total mental awareness. She was able to speak to those she loved and told them how she had loved them. Still in denial as the clock was ticking, I thought she would pull through once again. This time only a miracle could save her. Believing in miracles, I was praying for one.

A few days later I stopped all visits, even hospice. They were not comforting for her. Their advice was to give her morphine. Why? She was not in pain. Yeah, it was more about rushing the transition of death. All I could think about was, wow the finale was coming.

I called her doctor telling her I didn't want hospice. The doctor agreed and mentioned if there were any problems, to refer them back to her. She was an Egyptian doctor. She was a wonderful doctor, and a spiritual person as well. She once said to me, "Don't you believe in miracles?"

I decide not to share that time with any outsiders. Not wanting to let go. At one point she said, "Let me go." I knew the spirit of her mother and beloved family was present in the room. I spoke to them and asked that they give me more time with her. It had only been a couple of days now with her at home. They would have her for eternity, but I had only a short time left with her on earth. I could hear them saying ok, then the room became lighter and I was able to focus on whatever time we did have left together. We went on as nothing was happening, but we both knew.

We both started to get tired and by then I knew the transition through the veil of death was starting, her eye-sight was starting to go. She couldn't see the flowers anymore at the foot of her bed, that was a sign.

As I brought the flowers closer to her, she had a beautiful smile. I asked her if she could see the color of the flowers? She said, "No." We both knew then the moment was approaching. She couldn't see anymore. What she saw was a blur, as she explained it.

A few days went by then her last words, "Mirtha, Mirtha, Mirtha," in a faint tone. As I ran into the room, I could see that she had fully gone into the transition... The Veil of Death.

Caring for her and talking to her, letting her know how much I loved her. I was hugging and kissing her. I would not leave her alone, repeating to her the promise we had made to each other, that we would be together forever.

I gave her espresso. She knew it was her coffee. She loved it. I got a cotton ball and I soaked it in the espresso and gently rubbed it on her lips. We both knew it was getting close to the time for her to depart, she was telling me in so many ways. Being in a sound sleep, at one point, she sat up on the bed and said, "No." She no longer wanted the warm blanket. I was trying to keep her body warm, it was becoming cold. A fever came over her, it was rough to bring it down, and at that point it was time for me to let go. I didn't want the fever to make her to suffer a stroke.

It was then that I let her know that I was ready for her to leave. It was the saddest moment in my life. Her family was waiting for her, especially her mother whom she loved very much. She waited, knowing I was not ready yet. God seeing us through, I was not ready, but knew her mother was waiting too. I could not be selfish.

The time came for the finale. She let me know. I called her granddaughter Clara, named after her, into the room. It was time to say goodbye. Within seconds of kissing and hugging her, she took her last breath. Her spirit had left her body, God had taken her hand and reunited her with her own mother.

My mother Clara passed on February 18, 2011, at 11:43 pm. It was all over. The 9 years we had shared all flashed by as if it had only been minutes. I couldn't believe that she was gone. My prayers had been answered, all I ever prayed for was to be there when she passed, and I was. Another confirmation. Caregiving and being a caregiver, especially when the finale comes.

Time after time there have been numerous events in my life that without doubt, I know in my mind that there is another place where we go when we are done here on this Earth. It is apparent to me that what we do on earth does matter. Spiritual realm.

Just the other day I was reading a scripture, when I heard something fall in the kitchen. There is no possible way that a utensil could fall on its own. It was a bell like sound. I caught myself saying "Mama you dropped your spoon." As I got up to check, there was a spoon on the floor. Another confirmation that there is truth to the other side. During her last two years of life, she only ate with a spoon. As we remember those that have passed on to the other side, they will forever be in our hearts as was the way they touched us. Rest.

# XIII

# RECOVERY FROM BLOW
## Higher Forces Love of Life

### If I can do it, you can do it!

I had come to fully understand that when I left Florida I should have never looked back. The movie had just come out, and there I was catching a plane to Miami because my mother was in the hospital. George knowing this, was calling from jail. He was totally against the idea of me going with all that was going on. I refused to listen, for me it brought me peace and therefore recovery from the negative force. Envy, jealousy. Some of you will think it is not true or believe that it is not a real thing.

We must never stop dreaming. Make your mark on this planet. I am so glad that you are at this point, reading the last chapter. It has taken my knowledge and understanding of recovery to get to this point.

In the movie, the Americano gets out. He makes a deal with the United States government. It's the part where she is in the car and the next scene he is behind the plexiglass. The movie shows that we were there in prison on a visit. It did not happen in this order. By the time filming of the movie started, he was back in jail for the deal that went bad in Cape Cod. What should have followed was a court room scene where he is released. The scene was edited out of the movie due to legal matters. The part that wasn't seen, for all of those that thought I had put him back behind bars, I didn't.

In the movie, Kristina was the court reporter. We stayed in touch with George all throughout the movie. If you take the time to see the credits you will see Kristina Sunshine Jung's name in there.

Throughout the years, it's been about recovery from blow after blow.

Cleansings dating back to biblical days, affirmations, prayers, candle burning, herbs, and reaching for alternative healing methods. Calling to oneself spiritual guides for the body and mind. It has been my survival kit, doing away with the negative forces we encounter every day in or lives.

Balance between addiction and recovery. Recovering of the body first, knowing the spirit follows, thus saving the spirit for the journey of everlasting life. Recovery. Using easy to follow steps. This, not only for oneself, but also in finding help for those who are close to us. We give love and spend thousands of dollars in rehab, and after only a few months later, all that money, some as much as 40 thousand dollars, just to see that it didn't work.

At the end of this book you will have a web site to go to for reference. Continue traveling on this journey with us, it will allow you to get in touch with me, purchase items, or to know where and how. Years ago, when there were no natural health stores, and no one knew anything about organic, we were fully aware of its potential and benefits.

Working with oils, herbs, and candles scents in recovery can contribute to your inner desire. It can wake up those feelings that for so long have been buried in you or eating you alive, with guilt, despair, unworthy hate, and all the negative vibes when all we want to do is live in peace and comfort. Investing time and energy in these formulas, it has worked for me and I hope it works for you, to bring celebration of the spirit.

As we are growing up, either our parents, or grandparents, are teachers of the higher force. As a child, I was raised catholic. I went to catholic school. A good and expensive education taught by nuns in habits, and a priest. While growing up under the strict rules set forth by the church and their teachings, there was always this question that I often wondered about. It was the coming to the knowledge that the spirit lives eternally, even as the body dies. Therefore, it's the life of the body and the spirit. We all have a mission in life.

Through prayers, affirmations, and attending spiritual services. You must stop and THINK.

T, Is it true? H, is it helpful? I, is it inspiring? N, is it necessary? K, is it kind? The spirit within gives us the knowledge to think, feel, and know without doubting oneself. For those that can afford it, retreats. Some retreats offer free attendance.

I believe each energy has its own identity. Even though I have never seen God or Jesus, I know they live. As with the spirit, also within. All over the world the forces are at work. In and far, beyond the universe.

Beam me up Scottie.

Truth from up above. A higher plane, only the spirit lives eternally, for the mortal body lives only but a short time here on earth.

Devote one hour a week to read the scriptures handed down to us by the Prophets. They reveal so much of the present. Set aside time with your children and make it routine, it starts there. Teach them how to pray simple words, so their spirit grows with the energy that it gives. It was easier for those that took the time.

When you take time, you get to know who you, the spirit is, it also has come to you. The light does not mean dream. From these things you will gain a spiritual strength. The power of the forces, as the spirit is in one's home. Also avoid yelling, screaming, and shouting. These actions are not from a state of peace. Nothing in life can have that effect on us unless we allow it.

Higher power or higher force, whatever it is, you have been taught. I hope to share my love of life. I love you all for taking the time to read this book.

We are still alive after all the blows. Here are a few examples to get you started. Learn through the techniques that I have used. Apply them for a week to your everyday routine. I will make these steps as easy as ABC.

Learn to embrace freedom and joy in everyday of your life.

Love yourself, love your spirit, love the world. It all comes down to love. Hang on to the positive path that you will encounter. It is always best to start with cleansings of the house, the body, and your spirit.

Water being one of the elements. Rosemary is a wonderful herb, if you have any in your cabinets start there. Boil your water, add your herb. I use 2 cups of water to 1 tablespoon of rosemary. There is another way that is very easy too. If you have an old pair of pantyhose, or a white sock, cut the tip off enough to be able to tie it. Stuff the herb in and place under running water while in the shower along with a white candle. This cleansing is for healing. It helps remove negative forces.

Back in the biblical days before Christianity, herbs and oils were used to wash and rid oneself of impurity in the spirit. Pure messages start to come in crystal clear. Sharing my method with crack addicts, it worked for them, as a cleansing of the spirit and health.

At times, you think this won't work. Positive energy is about making it work. Through different types of meditation, I have come to settle the mind, getting in tune with the spirit. We are all caught up in a world full of modern technology. One way or another people bombard us every day. Telemarketers calling us at night when we get home. The neighbor's dog barking. For those that live in the big city, keeping the noise out. We are always around noise.

I started with meditation, not yoga. I would close my eyes and would place myself by a river with all my loved ones, having a picnic. I created the scene in my head. I did take some advice and started counseling. That, along with the techniques that I had, also applied for me while behind bars. You'd be surprised what can be used in that hell called prison. They could lock up your body, but they could not lock up your mind.

Humility is a beautiful inner feeling. How many of you know humility? One evening, as I was leaving San Francisco, for those of you that have not been there, you must put it on your wish list of places to see. The city by the bay. It is the most beautiful city I have ever seen. Magic of its own in the summer evenings. The weather, the ocean mist at night against your face. The chill of the night as you settle in. Anyhow, that evening, I was leaving. It was just before Thanksgiving. Everyone in the streets, leaving work with their bouquets of flowers to decorate their lavishing table. In front of me was this woman, and a homeless man. It saddened me to see how she truly was able to walk by him and totally ignore his beg for anything. She wouldn't even have given a flower from her fancy bouquets. As I approached the man. I had no flowers, it was going to be my first Thanksgiving without my family. I could not walk by him and look in his eyes, just to give thanks the next day. I gave him a dollar. He looked up at me and said, "Gods bless you." Just for that moment, he thought of God.

The following week I received a check that I didn't expect, it was for $250 dollars. What a blessing. I was so thankful that the higher power looked out after me and the homeless man. For out of his mouth came, God bless you. He had knowledge of the higher power.

I never knew what true happiness was, until I looked back. Looking back with hind sight that is, as they say is always 20/20. I now see what happiness really is. I call it love. How we feel free to, use it, abuse it, and then destroy it, along with the spirit.

As the years unfold one comes to the realization that... What a gift they all are. Love, peace, health, wealth, and happiness. Keeping the spirit alive and well. Happiness. It's true what they say, it can't be bought, you can't make someone happy. You can make them laugh, you can make them smile, and only we can embrace it. The gift that comes from the peace made with ones Higher Power. That is true happiness.

# CONCLUSION

A s the years have passed since the making of the movie BLOW. I will never forget Teddy. Recalling his words when he was alive, "Life will never be the same after this movie." It really did change my life. Not with money, because there was none. It was far more valuable realizing the spirit from beyond. Understanding the other side loud and clear. It was Teddy on the other side. "It's going to be alright."

Choices in the moment, choices under pressure. Desperation that sets in can cause a devastating aftermath, the spirit goes into shock as the light starts to dim. The spirits have shown me over and over, not to doubt the message nor the signs. Believe that God has the power to change us and help those in need. We are not alone, keep hope alive, and treasure love. It is through knowledge of mistakes and the choices we make that the light is to keep shinning. A reflection of our spirit. If the light goes out, then we have killed the spirit. Thus, becoming soulless.

Be awake and advise those who are not of the light. Listen to your feelings. If your body is healing along with spirit, the mind is in recovery too from whatever you've been blown away by.

We are given the ability to move on. No matter how negative things have been. Looking in the mirror now, seeing into my own eyes, and seeing the reflection looking back at me, knowing and believing that I am a great human. Repeating it over and over. Being happy with oneself.

I look at life so different now and I hope that you will to. From the crash behind bars through the edge of darkness, and hell on earth. Forgiveness means to be able to recover from any kind of blow.

I did away with the drugs, lifestyle, the craziness, and the pills. The escapes that we all go through, of one kind or another. We all have different reasons. Taking that first step is the recovery. Trying different techniques. Applying candles, herbs, oils, and things.

Know yourself, believe in yourself. No room for doubting yourself, allow no one to disrespect you, and value yourself.

Saving myself and those that want to be saved, focusing on the path of light, has given them and myself recovery.

Kristina had waited over 20 years to reunite with her father, staying in touch with him over the years. The time finally came for him to get out of prison. Georg asked her for help to relocate him on an early release to California. Kristina made arrangements with the F.B.I parole officer. She was interviewed and investigated.

Her father was granted permission to be released to her care, he could finally be brought to San Francisco for the overdue reunion with his heart and grandchildren. Another chance to be a father, and this time a grandfather.

She passed the investigation and background checks, then he was granted an early release and came out to California. Somehow TMZ already knew about his arrival. They were there to interview him, it was not a quiet affair. Right from the beginning, this was the exposure he was bringing.

He had a deadline to report to the halfway house. After reporting the following day, Kristina was excited to see her father for the first time in twenty years. She sees him, but the demons were out in force. While he was being housed at the half way house, Kristina would go back and forth. It was a 4 ½ hour drive round trip for her to get to him.

She was also dealing with her four children, yes George's grandchildren. After a few months at the halfway house, his paperwork was transferred. Now it was time to find him a place to live. Kristina went out and rented a beautiful 4-bedroom house for him, all in her name too. His parole officer had to make a visit to the house and inspect it. She needed to find it fit for him to come live and be fitted with an ankle bracelet. That process alone was insane.

Now on house arrest, with Kristina taking care of him, meanwhile dealing with the kids and her own life. There was no one there to help her at the time as they are now today, "helping him."

George constantly telling her that he would make it right. He was still having to report back to the halfway house under his terms and conditions. Once again, Kristina, having to travel 4 1/2 hours round trip, then waiting until he was done reporting. It was almost every day.

The day came when it was time to remove the ankle bracelet. They left the halfway house and returned home. Kristina was so happy now, they finally had the freedom to go out together.

Thanksgiving was the following day, she was sick at the time, so he suggested that she go home and rest, as he would be doing the same. He would see her tomorrow on Thanksgiving Day. That morning, Kristina goes to the house, walks in the room, and he was gone. At first, she thought he had been kidnapped, until she opens the closet door to find all the shirts, pants, and shoes that she bought him… GONE! What a blow for her, it was so saddening.

He used his daughter once again, this time to find a way out. He lied to her, and never showed up to their first Thanksgiving together after 20 years, he just left without a word.

Even her sister Clara, my daughter, betrayed us for George. She actually went to live with him in San Diego where they are now.

He has all these people surrounding him taking advantage of his short-term memory loss. Even attempting to make a docuseries that they want Kristina to be a part of. His dominatrix mistress played a major part in separating Kristina and her father. She did not want them to have any type of relationship whatsoever. I only have one question…

Where were these people with their good hearts when it was time to ask the F.B.I. for an early release for him? Why his daughter? To complicate matters, she was going through a horrible divorce at the same time.

Kristina is now free from both these men. One being her father, and the other one her ex. My prayers were answered.

Moving on, giving myself to the higher power. Every moment I take a breath, I am most grateful, and I bow my head down before thy and humbly give thanks for giving me the spirit to know and keep the truth in my heart stronger than ever. The strength to follow the light and stay on the path, never to return to the edge of darkness, or behind bars, but to share family time now and avoid blow after blow as so, not to relapse.

My being, in tune with the higher force, to reach eternal life through endurance and patience, making us a part of a new movement, beyond belief, to follow the plan when it all ends. The promise of eternal life is alive.

There is no other truth in my heart today. Only that of love. The love I have inside for God and his only begotten son, and the spirit that guides me through these times in my life, with all the love in the world for he is my example. Love! Love! Love! Never having any regrets. Staying on the path to recovery, living in the light.

IF I CAN DO IT… YOU CAN DO IT TOO!

# ACKNOWLEDGMENT

We thank all of you for sharing in our journey to recovery.

To all those that helped me finish this book. I love you. You know who you are.

Life is to be cherished and love is to be treasured.

Please visit my web site www.mirthajung.com

The End

Printed in the United States
By Bookmasters